D1074133

SPELL CORRECTLY

HERMAN F. BENTHUL
Former Assistant Superintendent, Curriculum Development
Dallas Public Schools
Dallas, Texas

EDNA A. ANDERSON
Superintendent of Schools
Laporte, Minnesota

ARLYS M. UTECH
Elementary Principal
Robbinsdale Area Public Schools
Robbinsdale, Minnesota

M. VIRGINIA BIGGY
Professor of Education
Department of Curriculum, College of Education
University of Lowell
Lowell, Massachusetts

BERYL LOFTMAN BAILEY
Former Professor of English
Hunter College
New York, New York

SILVER BURDETT COMPANY
Morristown, New Jersey • Glenview, Ill. • Palo Alto • Dallas • Atlanta

CONTENTS

We gratefully acknowledge the assistance and helpful recommendations of Major Armstead, Jr., of the Language Arts Mobile Laboratory of the Chicago Public Schools.

Illustrations by Al Fiorentino, George Buctel, H. B. Vestal Cover by Matt Greene, photograph by Henry Groskinsky

ISBN 0-382-03257-8

WHEN YOU STUDY A WORD

1. Say the word carefully. Hear the sounds in the word.

Does the word have more letters than sounds?

2. Notice how each sound in the word is spelled. Picture the word in your mind.

Is any sound spelled in a tricky way?

3. Think of other words that have the same spelling pattern as the one you are studying.

How many syllables does the word have?

Does the word have a suffix or a prefix?

4. Write the word and check your spelling. If you make a mistake, write the word correctly. Underline the part of the word that gives you trouble.

5. Read the meaning of the word in your Spelling Dictionary.

6. Write the word again. Can you write a sentence using the word?

IF YOU MISSPELL A WORD

Everyone misspells a word once in a while. To perfect your spelling ability, always analyze each error. Decide the probable cause for your misspelled word. How can you remedy the situation so that you won't make the mistake again? Here are a few reasons for misspellings and some suggestions to help you.

Why You Misspell	What You Can Do About It
1. You are not sure of the pronunciation of a word.	• Listen to your teacher pronounce the word. • Ask some friends to say the word; listen carefully. • Find the respelling of the word in the dictionary. Then say the word to yourself. Study the spelling.
2. Your handwriting is difficult to read. Even you have trouble reading it sometimes!	• Practice writing the letter or letters that are causing the trouble. Take pride in your writing. • Copy the word from the model in the word list. • Ask a friend to read your writing for legibility.
3. You write too quickly or too slowly. You leave out parts of words. Or you put in extra letters.	• Practice writing at a speed that allows you to form your letters well. • Get in the habit of looking at each word just for correct spelling. Every time you write something, proofread each word for correct spelling.
4. You aren't sure of the meaning of the word you are studying.	• Guess what the word means. Then find the word in your dictionary and verify its meaning. • Record the word in a notebook. Write several sentences showing different meanings of the word.
5. You can't remember which letters spell a sound in the word.	• If there is a rule about the sound and the letters, learn it and apply it. If a word is an exception to the rule, remember that. • Decide if the word is like any words you know. • Ask a classmate who can spell the word to give you a hint so that you can remember it.
6. The word is tricky and hard to remember.	• Figure out some way to remember the spelling. Maybe you can think of a "memory aid," such as this: ***Urge on the surgeon.***

Here are some special words to study each month. The pages called "When You Study a Word" and "If You Misspell a Word" should help you learn the words.

September (Sept.)

deceit conceit leisure
deceitful leisurely
receive seize
received seized
receiving seizing
receipt seizure
either neither ceilings

October (Oct.)

loose loosely
squarely purposely
privately sincerely
totally finally
originally actually
lonesome careful ninety
advisable decorative

November (Nov.)

caught haughty
taught daughter
slaughter naughty
ought bought fought
brought thought
thoughtful thoughtless
forethought afterthought

December (Dec.)

enjoy enjoys enjoyable
annoy annoyed annoying
employ employment
joy joyful joyous
reply replying replied
multiplying multiplied
satisfying satisfied

January (Jan.)

grown groan
border boarder
guessed guest
leased least
ceiling sealing
pedal peddle petal
medal meddle metal

February (Feb.)

calves halves knives
leaves loaves thieves
wives lives wolves
wharves shelves
myself yourself itself
ourselves themselves
yourselves

March (Mar.)

trail trial
bond bound
carton cartoon
attack attach
loose lose loss
later latter
formally formerly

April (Apr.)

cheerful cheerfulness
sudden suddenness
lonely loneliness
kindly kindliness
cave cavern cavernous
mountain mountainous
poison poisonous

May

badge edge bridge
fudge budget gadget
hedge ledge ridge
lodge lodger lodgings
pledge pledged pledging
judge judges judged
judging judgment

June

governor government
jewelry probably
grocery business
different difference
delivery deliveries
factory factories
memory memories

July and August (Aug.)

Remember to proofread everything you write in July and August—and in the other ten months, too. Try always to spell correctly.

1

Trust your dentist. The system used and the stuff put in your mouth are meant to increase the life of your teeth.

blank
draft
yell
neck
deaf
meant
print
socks
stock
trust
stuff
twelve
wealth
dentist
system
sympathy

SOUNDS and PATTERNS

1. Each word in the box begins and ends with a **consonant** sound and has one **short vowel** sound. Say each word. The symbol /a/ is read like this: the short *a* sound.

/a/	/e/	/i/	/o/	/u/
hat	pen	ring	clock	brush

Write the list words in which:

- **a.** /a/ is spelled with *a*
- **b.** /o/ is spelled with *o*
- **c.** /u/ is spelled with *u*
- **d.** /e/ is spelled with *e*

2. Each part of a word that has a vowel is a **syllable.** Write the two-syllable list word in which you hear both /e/ and /i/.

3. Write the words in which /i/ is spelled *y*. In which words is /i/ spelled *i*?

> Short vowels are usually spelled with *a, e, i, o,* or *u*. Sometimes /i/ is spelled *y*.

4. Write three list words in which /e/ is spelled with two letters.

STRUCTURE and MEANING

1. The simplest form of a word is the **base word.** A letter, or letters, added to a base word is a **suffix.** In the box a suffix has been added to a base word to form the past tense. Write the suffix that forms the past tense of *list*.

list + *ed* ⟶ listed

> The letters *ed* are often added to base words to form the past tense.

2. Write the past-tense form of each list word below.
   a. draft **b.** yell **c.** stuff

3. Complete each sentence with the *ed* form of a list word.
   a. This magazine was ___ on a special kind of paper.
   b. The shelves were ___ with canned goods.

4. Write the list word that completes the sentence below.
   I told Father, "I thought you ___ what you said yesterday."

5. A word that has about the same meaning as another word is called a **synonym.** Write a list word that is a synonym for:
   a. faith **b.** method **c.** empty **d.** pity **e.** dozen

6. ***DICTIONARY*** Turn to the Spelling Dictionary, page 116. Read the information about **entry words** and **guide words.**
   The guide words on one page of your Spelling Dictionary are *vacuum* and *yourself*. Write the list words that are entry words on that page. Write them in alphabetical order. Do not look in your Spelling Dictionary.

RIDDLES Use words from both lists.

7. Write the list word that answers each riddle below.
   a. I'm your friend. I keep your teeth healthy. Who am I?
   b. I describe a thick fog or forest. Which word am I?
   c. Bob trips over his own feet. Which word describes him?

blank
draft
yell
neck
deaf
meant
print
socks
stock
trust
stuff
twelve
wealth
dentist
system
sympathy

primitive
mammals
capture
clumsy
dense
docile
flint
glimpse
domesticate

a a a a
o o o o
sock draft

HANDWRITING Spelling errors are made when the letters *a* and *o* are not written carefully. Practice writing *a* and *o*. Be sure to bring *a* back to the line. Be sure to close *o*. Write *sock* and *draft*.

primitive
mammals
capture
clumsy
dense
docile
flint
glimpse
domesticate

CHECK POINT Get ready this minute!

A = *GAME TIME!*

WORD KNOWLEDGE

1. Write the missing words.

The picture shows a scene in (a) times. Both the man and tiger are classified as (b). Many weapons in this age were made of (c).

2. Write the list word that is a synonym for:

a. obedient **b.** awkward
c. quick look **d.** thick

3. Many English words came originally from Latin. Some of these words have changed in spelling and meaning.

Write the list word that comes from:

a. *primus* (first) **b.** *densus* (dense)
c. *capere* (seize) **d.** *domus* (house)

PROGRESS CHECK

WORD CHALLENGE

Look up the following words in a dictionary.

kangaroo *dog*
opossum *frog*
wombat *bandicoot*

a. List the words that name mammals.

b. Which word does not name a mammal? Tell why.

The high weight of the freight
Caused delay. We were late!
But we had to obey.
His claim for the rate
We hastened to pay.

2 The Vowel /ā/

SOUNDS and PATTERNS

1. In many words /ā/ is spelled in the **VC*e* pattern.** VC*e* means "vowel-consonant-*e*."

Write the list words in which /ā/ is spelled in the VC*e* pattern, as in *tame*.

2. Two adjoining letters that spell a single sound are called a **digraph.** Say the words shown in the box. In each word /ā/ is spelled with a digraph.

/ā/
main
day

a. Write list words in which /ā/ is spelled with the vowel digraph *ai*.

b. Write list words that end with /ā/. Underline the digraphs that spell /ā/.

3. A syllable that ends with a vowel is an **open syllable.** In the box a curved line is drawn under the open syllable.

fa mous

In which list words is /ā/ in an open syllable spelled with a single letter? Draw a curved line under the syllable.

> The most common ways of spelling /ā/ are in the VC*e* pattern, with a digraph, and with the letter *a* in an open syllable.

4. Write words in which /ā/ is spelled *eigh*.

claim
main
grain
waist
rate
blame
chase
favor
native
labor
delay
betray
weight
freight
obey
prey

claim
main
grain
waist
rate
blame
chase
favor
native
labor
delay
betray
weight
freight
obey
prey

STRUCTURE and MEANING

1. Write the *ed* form of the words in parentheses.

a. Our team was (favor) to win the championship.

b. We (claim) the highest number of points in the league.

2. Notice the past-tense forms at the right. Only the letter *d* is added to each base word.

name	hate
named	hated

Write the past-tense form of each word below.

a. chase **b.** rate **c.** blame

In spelling a past-tense form, the letters *ed* or *d* are often added to the base word. Sometimes the suffix *ed* adds a syllable.

3. Sometimes the suffix *ing* is added to a base word. Look at the word in the box. Then write the *ing* form of the list words below.

stray + *ing*→straying

a. delay **b.** obey **c.** labor

4. Words that have the same sounds but different meanings and spellings are called **homophones.** Write a homophone for:

a. pray **b.** mane **c.** waste **d.** wait

5. ***DICTIONARY*** Each entry word is followed by a **respelling.** The respelling has a symbol for each sound in the word. The marks above the vowel letters are **diacritical marks.** Study the Key to Pronunciation on page 116.

Write the list word for each respelling below.

a. (blām) **b.** (grān) **c.** (prā) **d.** (frāt)

vale
veil
stake
vane
vain
vein
traitor
stockade
reign

RHYMING WORDS Use words from both lists.

6. For each of the following words, write a rhyming word in which /ā/ is spelled a different way.

a. aim **b.** stray **c.** sale **d.** neighbor **e.** afraid **f.** gain

HANDWRITING Spelling errors are often caused by writing the letters *m* and *n* carelessly. Be sure to write each *m* with three humps. Write each *n* with two humps. Practice writing *main.*

m m m

n n

main

CHECK POINT Our neighbors were making a design as they laid the bricks in place. B

vale
veil
stake
vane
vain
vein
traitor
stockade
reign

WORD KNOWLEDGE

1. Write the list words needed to complete the following sentences.

The miner searched in (a) for a rich (b) of ore. The weather (c) on the shack was twisted by high winds. As dusk approached, a (d) of fog settled over the (e).

2. Write a homophone for each word below.
a. rain **b.** steak

3. Write a list word for each definition below.
a. an enclosure to confine people or animals
b. one guilty of treason

PROGRESS CHECK

WORD CHALLENGE
The words below refer to articles of clothing. Write a definition of each word. Then name the country or countries where each item might be most popular.
a. lederhosen **b.** caftan
c. kimono **d.** muumuu

3

Ben watched the theater screen in horror. The villain seized the secret formula. Ben grieved for the hero, trapped under the cheap steel ceiling.

steel
steep
speed
screen
deal
cheap
steam
least
hygiene
grieve
receive
ceiling
seize
secret
fever
theater

SOUNDS and PATTERNS

1. In which list words is /ē/ spelled with the following digraphs?

a. *ea* **b.** *ee*

2. Is *ea* in *theater* a vowel digraph? Explain.

3. Write three list words in which /ē/ is spelled with the letter *e* in the open syllable.

4. Write the words in which /ē/ is spelled *ie*.

5. Write the words in which /ē/ is spelled *ei*. Underline the consonant letter before *ei* in each word.

> The most common ways of spelling /ē/ are with the digraphs *ee, ea,* and *ie;* with the digraph *ei* after /s/; and with *e* in the open syllable.

6. Consonant sounds that come together in a word are called **consonant clusters.** A consonant cluster is always spelled with two or more consonant letters.

/kl/	claim
/mp/	lamp

Study the words shown in the box. Then write the list words that:

a. begin with a consonant cluster

b. end with a consonant cluster

STRUCTURE and MEANING

1. The suffix *er* is often added to a base word to form a word that compares two things. The suffix *er* can mean "more." Write the *er* form of a list word to complete this sentence about the picture:

The pen that costs 59¢ is ___ than the one that costs 89¢.

2. The suffix *est* is often added to a base word to form a word that compares more than two things. Complete each sentence with the *est* form of a list word.
   a. The pen that costs 39¢ is the ___ of all.
   b. I can pedal my bicycle up the ___ hill in town.

3. Which word means "smallest amount" in this sentence? The baby always eats the least of all.

4. The word in parentheses is a homophone for a list word. Write the list word that is correct for each blank.
   a. (steal) a ___ knife b. (seas) will ___ the thief

5. Write a list word for each meaning.
   a. to feel sad b. rules of health c. to capture

6. ***DICTIONARY*** This is a **stress mark:** (ʹ). The dictionary uses it in the respelling of a word to show which syllable to stress in pronouncing the word. Write the words below. Draw a curved line under the letters that spell the stressed syllable in each word. Check your dictionary.
   a. hygiene b. fever c. theater d. secret

steel
steep
speed
screen
deal
cheap
steam
least
hygiene
grieve
receive
ceiling
seize
secret
fever
theater

PROOFREADING Use words from both lists.

7. Four words in the paragraph below need suffixes to form the past tense. Write the correct form of each word.

Luisa compete in a contest. She receive an award for a story about a driver the police had seize three times. The driver had repeat the offense of speeding.

marquee
feature
scheme
routine
compete
mezzanine
jubilee
repeat
supreme

e l e l i
steel least
seize ceiling

HANDWRITING The letters *e*, *l*, and *i* must be written carefully. Loop *e* and *l*. Remember that *l* is tall. Do not loop *i*. Remember to dot *i*. Practice writing *steel, least, seize,* and *ceiling.*

marquee
feature
scheme
routine
compete
mezzanine
jubilee
repeat
supreme

CHECK POINT I don't believe it is easy to learn a piece of music in a week. Ⓒ

WORD KNOWLEDGE

1. Complete each sentence with a list word.

The theater (a) attracts many people. They will see two (b) films. One is a comedy; the other, a story of (c) courage.

2. Which word belongs with each group?

a. lobby, balcony, ____
b. celebration, festival, ____
c. plan, plot, ____
d. schedule, method, ____

3. Which list words rhyme with these words?

a. sweet **b.** gleam **c.** scene

PROGRESS CHECK

WORD CHALLENGE

Each word below describes a kind of theatrical performance. Write a word that tells who performs each of these acts:

a. acrobatics
b. pantomime
c. ballet
d. tragedy

The pilot, set for the flight,
Attendants, so polite,
Greeting people of every type.
Seat belts tight; ready to fly
To an island waiting to satisfy.

SOUNDS and PATTERNS

1. Say the words in the box. Listen for the vowel /ī/.

file
type
tight

a. Write the word in which /ī/ is spelled with the letter *i* in the VC*e* pattern.
b. Write the word in which /ī/ is spelled with the letter *y* in the VC*e* pattern.
c. In which word is /ī/ spelled *igh*?

2. Write list words that end with /ī/ spelled *y*.

> The /ī/ may be spelled *i* or *y* in the VC*e* pattern. The /ī/ at the end of a word is usually spelled *y*. Before /t/, the /ī/ is often spelled *igh*.

3. Write the list words in which /ī/ is spelled:
a. *i* in the VC*e* pattern
b. *y* in the VC*e* pattern

4. In which list words is /ī/ spelled *igh*?

5. The /ī/ in a stressed open syllable is often spelled with a single letter. Which list words illustrate this?

6. Write words that illustrate these sounds:
a. consonant clusters that begin words
b. the /ī/ that begins words

strike
wire
file
polite
type
style
pilot
climate
satisfy
reply
apply
aisle
island
tight
delighted
midnight

strike
wire
file
polite
type
style
pilot
climate
satisfy
reply
apply
aisle
island
tight
delighted
midnight

STRUCTURE and MEANING

1. Write the list word that is a past-tense spelling. Underline the suffix in the word.

2. Complete the sentence with the past tense of list words.
The secretary (a) the letter and (b) a copy.

3. The word *supplied* has two word parts: base word + past.
a. Which letter in *supply* is not in *supplied?*
b. Which letters in *supplied* are not in the base word?

If a word ends with *y* preceded by a consonant letter, the past tense is spelled by changing *y* to *i* and adding *ed.*

4. Write the past-tense form of each list word below.
a. apply **b.** reply **c.** satisfy

5. ***DICTIONARY*** In the respelling of an entry word, the pronunciation of a weak vowel is shown by the symbol **ə.** This symbol is called the **schwa.** Turn to the Key to Pronunciation on page 116. Notice the letters that spell /ə/.
Write list words for the following respellings.
a. (pī′ lət) **b.** (pə līt′) **c.** (ə plī′) **d.** (ī′ lənd)

PUZZLE Use words from both lists.

dive
glide
tidal
hydroplane
hydrofoil
maritime
bayou
capsize
gyroscope

6. Copy and complete the puzzle.

Across
1. yearly weather
4. courteous
6. passageway

Down
1. turn over
2. body of land surrounded by water
3. move smoothly
5. having tides

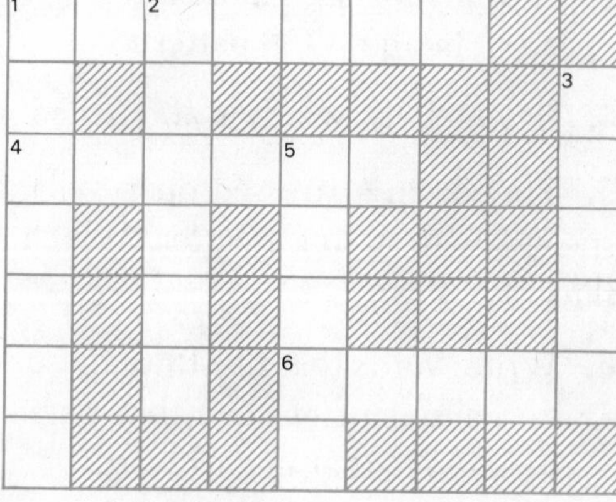

HANDWRITING Be sure the letter *d* does not look like *cl*. Close the letter *d*. Practice writing *d* and *cl*. Then write the words *delight* and *climate*. Now practice writing other words that begin with the letter *d*.

d cl cl d

delight

climate

CHECK POINT Let's try to divide the work tonight so none of us will get too tired. **D**

dive
glide
tidal
hydroplane
hydrofoil
maritime
bayou
capsize
gyroscope

WORD KNOWLEDGE

1. Picture **a** shows a hydroplane; picture **b**, a hydrofoil. Write the name of each boat. Underline the part of each word that comes from the Greek word *hydor*, meaning "water."

2. Which list word names an instrument found on a ship? Write the letter of the description below that tells what this instrument does.

- **a.** collects weather information
- **b.** keeps the ship balanced

3. Which word best completes each sentence?

- **a.** A huge ____ wave swept over the boat.
- **b.** We saw the boat ____ in the wave.
- **c.** A sailplane can ____ for many miles.
- **d.** Some birds ____ into the water for fish.
- **e.** Laws governing the sea are ____ laws.
- **f.** A ____ is a marshy body of water.

PROGRESS CHECK

WORD CHALLENGE

Many English words begin with prefixes that come from the Latin word *aqua* and the Greek word *hydor*. Both words mean "water." The prefixes may be spelled differently in different words.

Write as many words as you can that come from these two words.

The Vowel /ō/

5

The fellow at the piano
Stole the show.
Rock 'n' roll, loads of soul,
A radio program was his goal.

moment
program
roller
postpone
throat
roast
owner
shown
fellow
narrow
soda
poultry
shoulder
boulder
radio
piano

SOUNDS and PATTERNS

1. Say the words in the box. Notice that /ō/ is spelled with a digraph in each word.

/ō/ roast, owner, poultry

Write list words in which /ō/ is spelled with a digraph. Underline the letters that spell /ō/.

2. Write the words that end with /ō/ spelled with a single letter.

3. Write the words in which /ō/ in a stressed open syllable is spelled with the letter *o*.

The /ō/ is most commonly spelled in the VC*e* pattern; with the digraphs *oa*, *ow*, and *ou*; and with *o* in a stressed open syllable.

4. Write the word *postpone*.

a. Draw a curved line under the letters in *postpone* that spell each syllable.

b. In each syllable of *postpone*, do you hear a vowel, or a consonant, after /ō/?

Any syllable that ends with a consonant sound is a **closed syllable.**

5. Write the homophone for each word.

a. bolder **b.** shone

STRUCTURE and MEANING

1. The suffix *er* can mean "one who" or "that which":

farmer (one who farms) *marker* (that which marks)

Write the list word for each meaning below.

a. one who owns **b.** that which rolls

2. Words that mean "more than one" are called **plural forms.** Say the plural forms shown in the box.

a. Write the word that ends with /z/, the last sound in *his.*

b. Write the word that ends with /s/, the last sound in *gets.*

moments
owners

Plural forms may end with /s/ or /z/. Both of these sounds may be spelled with the letter *s.*

3. Write words for the respellings below.

a. (prō′ gramz) **b.** (sō′ dəz) **c.** (fel′ ōz) **d.** (rōsts)

4. Write the *ed* form of *show* to complete this sentence:

The picture ____ a dome over a city.

5. Use a list word to complete this sentence:

Our class has been ____ many interesting films this year.

6. ***DICTIONARY*** Some words have more than one meaning. In a dictionary, each different meaning is numbered. Study the example on page 116.

Look up the word *shoulder* in your Spelling Dictionary. Write the numeral for the definition that matches the use of *shoulder* in the sentence below.

John drove his car onto the soft shoulder.

RIDDLES Use words from both lists.

7. Read each clue. Write the word that answers each riddle.

a. a boy, not a girl **b.** has "bone" but no muscle

c. sung by one, never two **d.** has wings but no fins

moment
program
roller
postpone
throat
roast
owner
shown
fellow
narrow
soda
poultry
shoulder
boulder
radio
piano

alto
soprano
solo
compose
trombone
oboe
bugle
duet
trio

u w u w
owner
shoulder

HANDWRITING The letters *u* and *w* look very much alike. Be careful when joining *u* and *w* to another letter in a word. Practice writing *u* and *w*. Then write the words *owner* and *shoulder*.

alto
soprano
solo
compose
trombone
oboe
bugle
duet
trio

CHECK POINT Did you know he once wrote some poems? **E**

WORD KNOWLEDGE

1. Write the list word that names each instrument described below. Then check your answers with your Spelling Dictionary.

a. This instrument was first made from the horn of an ox. Its name comes from the Latin word *buculus*, meaning "ox."

b. It looks somewhat like a trumpet. Its name comes from the Italian word *tromba*, meaning "trumpet."

c. This woodwind was once called a *hautboy*, meaning "high wood." It is a woodwind instrument with a high tone.

2. Write the list word that names a musical group made up of the following numbers.

a. one **b.** two **c.** three

3. Which word names each voice below?

a. highest singing voice

b. second highest singing voice

4. Which list word comes from the prefix *com*, meaning "together," and the French word *poser*, meaning "to place"?

PROGRESS CHECK

WORD CHALLENGE

The Latin words *unus* (one), *duo* (two), and *tres* (three) are used in forming many words.

a. Write each of the following and give its meaning.

unicorn *duplex* *triangle*

b. Make a list of words that come from *unus, duo, tres.*

6 REVIEW and EXTENSION

The words in the boxes below are words you have studied. If you can spell them, you will have no trouble spelling the new list words. The new list words have patterns that you know.

SOUNDS and PATTERNS

1. Say each word below. Hear the short vowel sounds.

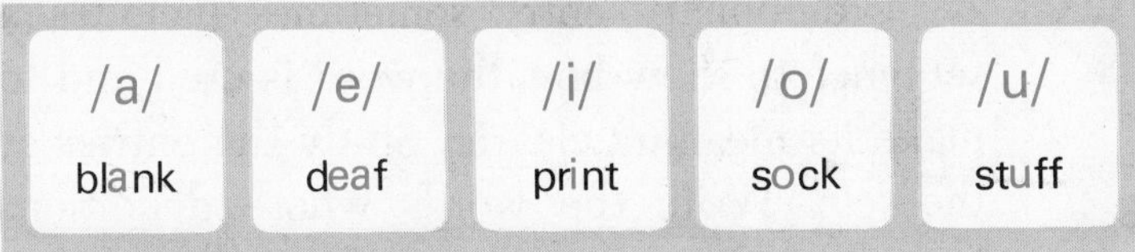

/a/	/e/	/i/	/o/	/u/
blank	deaf	print	sock	stuff

Write the list words of one syllable in which you hear these short vowel sounds:

a. /i/ **b.** /a/ **c.** /u/

2. The box below shows spelling patterns for the long vowel sounds. Study these patterns.

VC<u>e</u> Pattern	Open Syllable	Vowel Digraph
/ā/ rate	/ā/ favor	/ā/ main delay
/ī/ wire	/ī/ pilot	/ō/ roast shown
/ō/ stone	/ō/ moment	/ē/ deal grieve

a. In which new list words do you see VC*e*?

b. Which new words contain a vowel digraph?

3. In four new list words, the first stressed syllable is an open syllable. Write the words.

4. Study the patterns that spell /ī/ in the box. Write a list word that shows each pattern.

/ī/	tight satisfy

5. Four list words begin with consonant clusters. Write these four words.

tank
bump
mint
stuck

gain
crate
railway
basin

seek
beads
deed
grief

desire
highway
magnify
silent

tone
toast
flown
token

ba sin (bā′ sən), *n.* 1. A shallow bowl used for washing. 2. All of the land drained by a river.

claim (klām), *v.* 1. To demand as one's right. The United States *claims* part of Antarctica. 2. To state. They *claim* they saw robbers.

draft (draft, dräft), *n.* 1. A current of air. 2. The selection of people to serve in an army. 3. A plan; a sketch. I made three different *drafts* of my speech.

–er[1], *adj.* or *adv. suffix.* Used for comparative forms. More.

–er[2], *n. suffix.* A person who; a thing that; that which.

print (print), *v.* To make copies from type. **—printer,** *n.* One engaged in printing.

steep (stēp), *adj.*, **steeper, steepest.** 1. Sloping sharply, almost straight up or down. 2. High.

tank (tangk), *n.* 1. A large container for liquids. 2. A military vehicle covered with armor and running on caterpillar tracks.

DICTIONARY

1. The entry word and its respelling are missing in the dictionary entry below. Read the definition. Then write the missing entry word.

——— (———), *n.* Twelve o'clock at night, when one day ends and a new day begins.

2. A dictionary entry sometimes includes a sentence to show how the word is used and to make its meaning clearer. Study the entries at the left. Write the words whose definitions include such sentences.

3. From the entries at the left, find and write the word that names the pictured object. Then write the numeral for the dictionary meaning that you used.

4. Write the word that has two syllables. Draw a curved line under the letters that spell the stressed syllable.

5. Notice the two entries for the suffix *er*. Each entry has a different meaning. These suffixes are used to make other forms of entry words.

a. Write *printer*. Then write *1* or *2* to show which *er* suffix was added to *print*.

b. Write *steeper*. Then write *1* or *2* to show which *er* suffix was added to *steep*.

CHECK POINT

If you misspelled words in Units 1–5, decide why you made errors. Study those words again. Then study the new words.

WORD STRUCTURE

1. Say each word below. Listen for the sound of *s*.

a. Which list words end with /z/ spelled *s*?
b. Which list words end with /s/ spelled *s*?

2. Study the past-tense forms below.

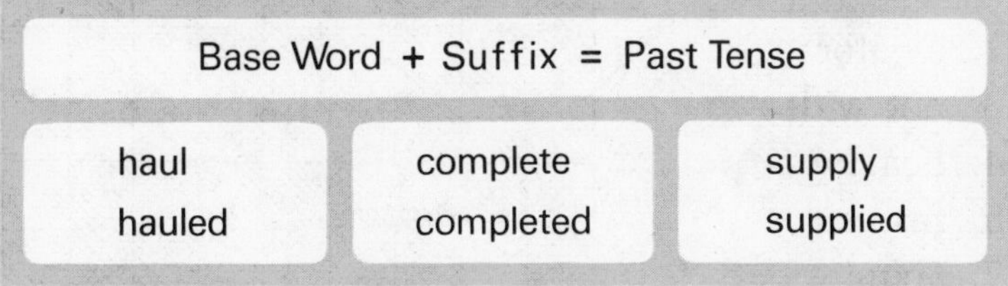

Base Word + Suffix = Past Tense
haul
hauled
complete
completed
supply
supplied

Which words are past-tense forms of these words?
a. roast **b.** gain **c.** magnify **d.** seize **e.** style

3. Which list word is a past-tense form of *fly*?

4. Notice the *ing* form of the word in the box. Write list words that are *ing* forms of *seek* and *speed*.

toast
toasting

5. Study the two meanings of the suffix *er* below.

"one who"		"that which"	
report	reporter	mark	marker

Write list words that mean:
a. one who prints **b.** that which bumps
c. that which toasts

tanks
tones
weights
radios
shoulders
gained
roasted
seized
magnified
styled
flown
speeding
seeking
bumper
printer
toaster

pilot
native
file
trust
style
narrow
wealth
gain
weight
theater
secret
betray
piano
grain
program
midnight
throat

PROGRESS CHECK

Be sure you can spell all the words in the first lists from Units 1–6.

ON YOUR OWN

1. Complete the puzzle with list words.

Across

2. middle of night
6. front of neck
8. riches
9. inborn

Down

1. aviator
3. not wide
4. heaviness
5. fashion
7. acquire

2. Write the words that complete the sentences.

a. The children will ____ out of the room.
b. They will harvest the ____ before winter.
c. The ____ was held in the ____.
d. We can ____ them not to ____ the ____.

scheme
compose
domesticate
mammals
veil
docile
capsize

3. Which words rhyme with those in italics?
In early times, there existed such ____
As mammoths, huge beavers, and even wild *camels*.
A mammoth was never inclined to be ____.
If careless, a hunter could end as a *fossil*.

4. Write the word that is a synonym for:

a. tame **b.** calm
c. cover **d.** plan

7 The Vowels /är/ and /ãr/

Pardon your parents if they guard you like kindergartners. Remember that you are their primary charge. Don't be alarmed — it's only temporary.

charge
charter
pardon
article
regards
kindergarten
guard
starch
lifeguard
scarce
various
parents
temporary
dictionary
library
primary

SOUNDS and PATTERNS

1. Say the words in the box. The curved line under each symbol shows that the letters stand for just one sound. This is the ***r*-controlled vowel** sound.

/är/	/ãr/	/er/
far	vary	January

a. Write three list words in which /ãr/, as in *vary*, is spelled *ar*.
b. Write nine list words in which /är/, as in *far*, is spelled *ar*.
c. Write four list words in which /er/, as in *January*, is spelled *ar*.

The /är/, /ãr/, and /er/ are often spelled with the letters *ar*.

2. Write words for the respellings below. Draw a curved line under the letters that spell each stressed syllable.

a. (ri gärdz′) **b.** (är′ tə kəl)
c. (pãr′ ənts) **d.** (vãr′ ē əs)

3. Write the word for this respelling: (lī′ brer ē). Underline the letters that spell the consonant cluster.

charge
charter
pardon
article
regards
kindergarten
guard
starch
lifeguard
scarce
various
parents
temporary
dictionary
library
primary

STRUCTURE and MEANING

1. Write a list word that can be used in place of each italicized word or phrase.

Our parents wrote the mayor a letter about the most recent *grant giving the rights* for a playground. Their *main* purpose was to tell about the *different kinds of* needs for a playground. They said money would be *in short supply*. The playground would not be a *short-term* improvement. They signed the letter with *good wishes*.

2. A word that is formed from two or more words is a **compound.** Write the compound that means "one who guards the life of a swimmer."

story + plural ⟶ stories
pony + plural ⟶ ponies

3. Each base word in the box ends with *y* preceded by a consonant letter.

a. Which letter in each base word is not in the plural?
b. Which letters in the plural are not in the base word?

In spelling the plural form of words that end with *y* preceded by a consonant letter, change the *y* to *i* and add *es*.

4. Write the plural form of each word below.

a. dictionary **b.** library

bombard
hearty
hardy
discharge
sergeant
armor
arsenal
blare
flare

5. Write the list word that comes from two German words—*kinder,* meaning "children," and *garten,* meaning "garden."

6. ***DICTIONARY*** Find *library* in your Spelling Dictionary. The information in brackets ([ ]) tells the origin of the word. What did the original Latin word mean?

GROUPS OF WORDS Use words from both lists.

7. Write a list word to complete each group of words.

a. private, corporal, ____ **b.** whistle, screech, ____
c. warehouse, armory, ____ **d.** thing, object, ____

HANDWRITING Notice how *or* and *ar* are written. Bring *a* back to the line before joining it to *r*. Close *o* and join it to *r* high above the line. Practice writing *or* and *ar*. Then write the words *armor* and *temporary*.

or ar or ar

armor

temporary

CHECK POINT Where could I buy a card table for my apartment? F

WORD KNOWLEDGE

1. Complete these comparisons with list words:

a. A lieutenant is to a captain as a corporal is to a ____.

b. Money is to a vault as ammunition is to an ____.

c. A release is to a prisoner as a ____ is to a soldier.

2. Which word means "to flame up briefly"?

3. Write *hearty* or *hardy* to complete each blank correctly.

a. ____ plants **b.** ____ laugh

4. Which list words complete the paragraph below?

In medieval times soldiers wore (a). They threw huge stones from a cannon called a (b). In the court the (c) of trumpets told of victory.

PROGRESS CHECK

bombard
hearty
hardy
discharge
sergeant
armor
arsenal
blare
flare

WORD CHALLENGE

Two kinds of agreements between nations at war are a *truce* and a *treaty*.

Look up these two words. Write the meaning of each word.

8

It is certain that it takes courage to research our urban problems. But if we further our efforts, we can furnish some answers to serve more people.

City Map

serve
observe
certain
curtain
furnish
furnace
further
urban
curfew
earnest
research
journey
journal
nourish
courage
courtesy

SOUNDS and PATTERNS

1. Say the word in the box. Notice the letters that spell /ėr/.

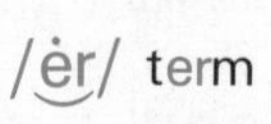

In which list words is /ėr/ spelled with *er*?

2. Which letters spell /ėr/ in each word below?
a. nurse **b.** learn

3. In which list words is /ėr/ spelled as in
a. learn? **b.** nurse?

4. Write the word for this respelling: (jėr′nē). Underline the letters by which /ėr/ is spelled.

5. Write the other list words in which /ėr/ is spelled as in *journey*.

> Two common ways /ėr/ is spelled are with the letters *er* and *ur*. Sometimes /ėr/ is spelled with the letters *ear* and *our*.

6. Which letters represent /s/ in these words?
a. serve **b.** certain

7. Write the two list words in which /s/ is spelled with the letter *c*.

8. Write the list words for these respellings:
a. (kėr′ ij) **b.** (jėr′ nəl)
Underline the letters that spell /j/.

STRUCTURE and MEANING

1. Which list word is a synonym for each of the following?
   a. trip **b.** window covering **c.** magazine

2. Words that have opposite meanings are **antonyms.** Write a list word that is an antonym for each word below.
   a. rural **b.** rudeness **c.** cowardice

3. A **prefix** may be used at the beginning of a base word to form another word. The prefix *un* means "not," and it can be used to form an antonym of the base word. Change each word in parentheses, using the prefix *un.*
   a. I'm (certain) of the time. **b.** The room is (furnished).

> Antonyms of some words may be formed by using a prefix meaning "not" with a base word.

4. In the Middle Ages a bell was rung each evening to tell the peasants to cover the fires for the night. The name of this signal comes from the French words *couvrir* (to cover) and *feu* (fire). We use this word now to mean a signal to come in from the streets. Write the word.

5. ***DICTIONARY*** The abbreviation *Ant.* after a definition in the dictionary means "antonym." Write an antonym for each of the following words. Use your Spelling Dictionary.
   a. certain **b.** nourish **c.** earnest

serve
observe
certain
curtain
furnish
furnace
further
urban
curfew
earnest
research
journey
journal
nourish
courage
courtesy

DOUBLETS Use words from both lists.

6. One of two different words that come from the same source is a **doublet.** The doublet of *servant* is *sergeant* because both words come from the French *servir,* meaning "to serve."
   Write a doublet for each of the following words.
   a. journal, from *diurnus,* meaning "daily"
   b. trouble, from *turba,* meaning "confusion"
   c. furniture, from *fournir,* meaning "to furnish"

flurry
whirlwind
hurricane
typhoon
earthquake
tornado
thermometer
torrent
turbulent

j j f f
further
journey

HANDWRITING The letters *j* and *f* look somewhat alike. The letter *j* loops below the line. The letter *f* loops below and above the line. Practice writing *j* and *f*. Then write *further* and *journey*.

flurry
whirlwind
hurricane
typhoon
earthquake
tornado
thermometer
torrent
turbulent

CHECK POINT I heard her tell my uncle to come early to purchase shoes. Ⓖ

WORD KNOWLEDGE

1. Which words complete the comparisons?
   a. *typhoon* or *hurricane?* A ____ is to the Atlantic as a ____ is to the Pacific.
   b. *whirlwind* or *tornado?* A flurry is to a blizzard as a ____ is to a ____.
2. Write the word that completes each phrase.
   a. ____ of rain **b.** ____ of snow
3. Write the word that fits each definition.
   a. an instrument for measuring temperature
   b. a trembling of the earth
   c. violent

WORD CHALLENGE

The instruments shown in the picture measure changes in weather. Write each word and after it the letter of the matching picture. Then tell what each instrument measures. Use a dictionary if you need help.

barometer *anemometer*
psychrometer *clinometer*

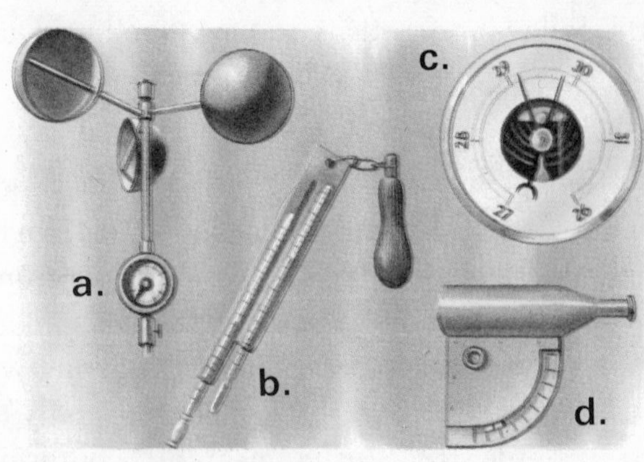

PROGRESS CHECK

Words can be used
As a source of force
By lawyers who appear in court,
Or by authors for their own support.

9 The Vowels /ôr/ and /ô/

SOUNDS and PATTERNS

1. Say the picture word. Hear the /ôr/. In which list words is /ôr/ spelled with *or*? Draw a curved line under the letters that spell the stressed syllable in words of more than one syllable.

> The /ôr/ is usually spelled *or*. In words of more than one syllable, /ôr/ is usually in a stressed syllable.

2. Write the homophone of *morn*. Underline the letters that spell /ôr/. Then write the other list words in which /ôr/ is spelled with *our*.

3. Say *form* and *fawn*. Say *fawn* and *autumn*. Notice the letters that spell /ô/.

/ôr/	form
/ô/	fawn autumn

a. In which list words is /ô/ spelled with *aw*?

b. In which words is /ô/ spelled with *au*?

4. Write list words for the respellings below.

a. (ôt) **b.** (fôt)

> The /ô/ may be spelled *au, aw,* or *ough* as well as with *o, a,* or *augh.*

fort
forth
force
court
mourn
source
border
orchard
support
according
ought
fought
fault
author
dawn
lawyer

fort
forth
force
court
mourn
source
border
orchard
support
according
ought
fought
fault
author
dawn
lawyer

STRUCTURE and MEANING

1. Write the homophone for each word below.

a. fourth **b.** morn **c.** boarder

2. Write the list word that means "one who practices law."

3. Add the correct suffix to a word to fit each definition.

a. one who mourns **b.** one who supports

4. Use list words to complete the paragraph below.

The (a) was located near the Mexican (b). Several battles were (c) there. A United States cavalry (d) was a (e) of protection for settlers.

5. ***DICTIONARY*** Look up *court* in your Spelling Dictionary. The abbreviations *n.* and *v.* in the entry mean *noun* and *verb.*

Look up *forth.* What abbreviation is used to show that *forth* is an adverb?

PUZZLE

Use words from both lists.

laurel
sycamore
balsa
catalpa
lumbermen
forestry
forester
reforestation
arbor

6. Copy and complete the puzzle.

Across

1. past of *fight*
3. military stronghold
4. edge
5. flowering tree
6. shade tree

Down

1. science of growing trees
2. kind of shrub
3. power; strength
4. a tree with light wood

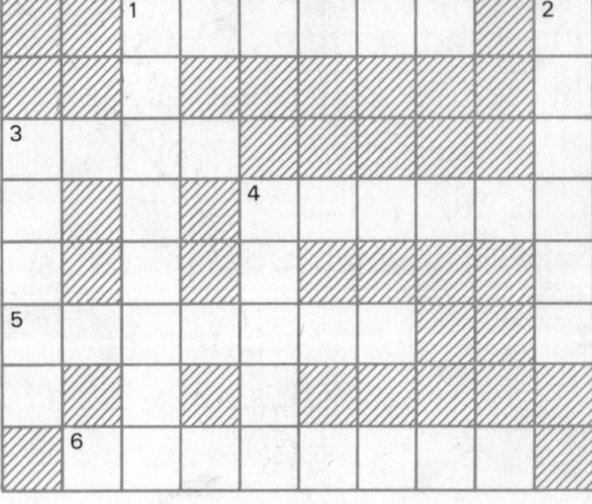

HANDWRITING The letter *p* is pointed at the top and looped below the line. The letter g begins as an oval and loops below the line. Practice writing *p, pp,* and *g*. Then write *support* and *fought*.

p pp g
support
fought

CHECK POINT I said I thought four boys were coming on Tuesday to haul away the corn.

laurel
sycamore
balsa
catalpa
lumbermen
forestry
forester
reforestation
arbor

WORD KNOWLEDGE

1. Write the missing words.

The picture shows a (a) marking the trees to be cut. Later, (b) will come to fell the trees. Then, to be sure that future generations have wood supplies, the (c) begins. Each kind of work is a part of the science of (d).

2. Write the words that name trees.

3. Write the word that names both a tree and a shrub.

4. President Franklin Roosevelt once called himself a "tree farmer." Write the list word he might have used in place of each word below.

a. farmer **b.** replanting

5. Write the compound word in the list.

6. In an arboretum, trees are grown for scientific purposes. Write the list word that is the base word of *arboretum*.

PROGRESS CHECK

WORD CHALLENGE

1. For each of the following, write a homophone that is the name of a tree.

a. beach **b.** fur **c.** plumb
d. seeder **e.** you **f.** pair

2. Look up *tamarack, ginkgo,* and *chinquapin* in a dictionary. Write a short description of each of these trees.

The Vowels /ou/ and /oi/ 10

You're bound to be annoyed if you get poison ivy. If you cannot avoid woodsy places, promptly take a soapy shower and then dry yourself with a clean towel.

bound
surround
amount
fountain
bounce
sour
towel
shower
coward
annoy
employ
oyster
avoid
poison
embroidery
appoint

SOUNDS and PATTERNS

1. Say *bond* and *bound*. In which word do you hear a vowel that sounds almost like two vowels?

2. Look at the words in the box. With which letters is /ou/ spelled in *bound*? in *towel*?

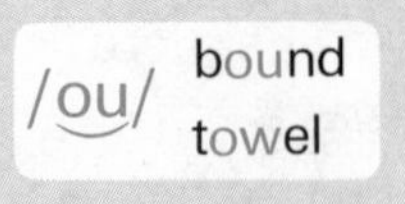

A vowel spelled with two letters that sound almost like two vowels is a **diphthong.**

3. Say *pint* and *point*. In which word do you hear a diphthong? Write the letters that stand for the diphthong in *avoid*.

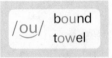

/oi/ avoid

4. Write list words that have these spellings:

a. /ou/ spelled with the letters *ow*
b. /ou/ spelled with the letters *ou*
c. /oi/ spelled with the letters *oi*
d. /oi/ spelled with *oy* at the end of a word

5. Write another word in which /oi/ is spelled with the letters *oy*.

The /ou/ diphthong is usually spelled with the letters *ou* or *ow*. The /oi/ diphthong is usually spelled with *oi* in the middle of a word and with *oy* at the end of a word.

STRUCTURE and MEANING

1. The suffix *ment,* meaning "the act of," forms a noun when it is added to a verb: *entertain* + *ment* ⟶ entertainment. Add the suffix *ment* to list words to complete these sentences:

a. Make your dental ___ early.

b. The factory offers full ___.

2. Read the paragraph below. Each italicized word can be replaced by a list word used with a suffix. Write the correct form of the list words that can be used.

The executive was very *disturbed* by the endless details of the reports that *encircled* him. At first, there seemed to be no way of *escaping* the great amount of paper work. But by the end of the week, he had *hired* someone to help him.

3. ***DICTIONARY*** Your dictionary has four different numbered entries for *bound. Bound* has four separate entries because it has four different histories.

Each italicized word or phrase below is a different meaning of *bound.* From your Spelling Dictionary, write the numeral of the entry that fits each meaning of *bound.*

Our school was *headed for* the football championship. We thought we were *sure* to win. The quarterback on the other team threw the ball high. Our safety took one great *leap* to get it. But the ball went out of *the boundary lines.*

PROOFREADING — Use words from both lists.

4. Write each word correctly by supplying letters for the blanks. Underline the letters that spell the diphthong in each word.

If you say no to a dare to sip a small am__ __nt of p__ __son, you are not a c__ __ard. Some sc__ __ndrel is trying to ann__ __ you. The suggestion is __ __trageous.

bound
surround
amount
fountain
bounce
sour
towel
shower
coward
annoy
employ
oyster
avoid
poison
embroidery
appoint

coy
dour
outrageous
poise
astounded
encounter
cowardice
scoundrel
buoyant

oun own

amount

coward

HANDWRITING Make sure that the letters *oun* do not look like *own*. The *u* ends with a downward stroke. The *w* ends with an upward stroke. Practice writing *oun* and *own.* Then write *amount* and *coward*.

coy
dour
outrageous
poise
astounded
encounter
cowardice
scoundrel
buoyant

CHECK POINT Now we make a point of enjoying every hour that we spend in the country. I

WORD KNOWLEDGE

1. Write the list words that have the meanings below.

a. pretending to be shy **b.** gloomy
c. energetic and happy **d.** shocking

2. Write the missing list words.

The sheriff never tried to avoid a dangerous (a) with a troublemaking (b). In fact, the sheriff always acted so swiftly that he (c) the lawbreaker. No one could ever accuse the sheriff of (d).

3. Complete the sentence with a list word.

It takes practice to gain ____ on the stage.

PROGRESS CHECK

WORD CHALLENGE

The words below could be used to describe storybook characters. Find the meaning of each word in a dictionary.

Write a sentence in which you use each word.

a. humane b. pacific
c. timorous d. dogmatic
e. shrewd f. rebellious

11 The Vowels /ü/ and /yü/

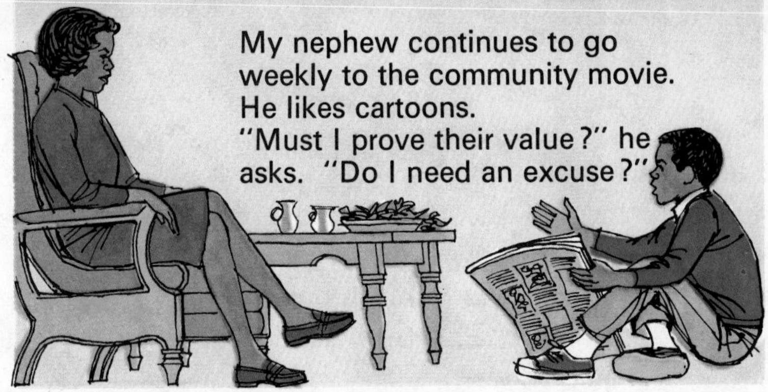

My nephew continues to go
weekly to the community movie.
He likes cartoons.
"Must I prove their value?" he
asks. "Do I need an excuse?"

SOUNDS and PATTERNS

/ü/ spoon

1. Notice the digraph that spells /ü/ in *spoon*. Write list words in which /ü/ is spelled with the digraph *oo*.

The /ü/ is usually spelled by the digraph *oo*.

/yü/ humid

2. Say the word in the box.
   a. With which letter is /yü/ spelled in *humid?*
   b. Is the /yü/ in *humid* in an open syllable?
   c. Write the list words in which /yü/ in an open syllable is spelled with the letter *u*.

3. Write the list words in which /yü/ is spelled in the VC*e* pattern.

4. Which words end with /yü/?

The most common ways /yü/ is spelled are
—with *u* in an open syllable, as in *music;*
—with *u* in the VC*e* pattern, as in *huge;*
—with the digraphs *ew* and *ue* at the end of words, as in *few* and *cue.*

5. In which list words is /ü/ spelled
   a. with the letter *o* in the VC*e* pattern?
   b. with the single letter *o?*

smooth
cartoon
proof
prove
improve
human
community
cute
confuse
excuse
value
continue
nephew
review
whom
movie

smooth
cartoon
proof
prove
improve
human
community
cute
confuse
excuse
value
continue
nephew
review
whom
movie

STRUCTURE and MEANING

1. Write the *er* or *est* form of the word in parentheses to correctly complete each sentence.

a. (smooth) Dionne is the ____ talker in our class.
b. (cute) The kitten is much ____ than the pet rabbit.

2. Write the common meaning for the prefixes *un, dis,* and *in.* Use your Spelling Dictionary.

3. Use the correct prefix with a list word, or a form of a list word, to replace the italicized words in each sentence.

a. The company will *not continue* polluting the air.
b. The condition of our streets is *not improved.*
c. Ignoring a way to prevent dirty air is *not human.*

4. ***DICTIONARY*** Pairs of words that have the same spellings but different pronunciations and different meanings are **homographs.** Homographs that come from the same source are listed under one entry in your Spelling Dictionary. Each pronunciation shows the part of speech that matches the pronunciation, as in the example below.

> **pre sent** (*v.* pri zent′; *n.* prez′ ənt), *v.* To give; offer. —*n.* A thing given; gift.

pudding
custard
dumpling
dessert
menu
recipe
chef
cutlery
cucumber

Look up *excuse* in your Spelling Dictionary. Read each sentence below. Which part of speech matches the pronunciation of *excuse* in each sentence?

a. Let's excuse Bob. **b.** He has an excellent excuse.

IMPROVING WORD USAGE Use words from both lists.

5. Choose another word for each italicized word or phrase.
The *cook* will *study again* the *directions* for the stew.
She told her *sister's son* to *go on* sharpening the *knives.*

HANDWRITING The beginning stroke of the letters *m, x,* and *v* is rounded. Notice where the final stroke of *v* ends. Practice writing *m, x,* and *v*. Be sure to cross *x*. Then write *movie* and *excuse*.

m x v

movie

excuse

CHECK POINT I knew they often used blue paint for swimming pools. J

pudding
custard
dumpling
dessert
menu
recipe
chef
cutlery
cucumber

WORD KNOWLEDGE

1. Complete the following comparisons.

a. A road map is to a traveler as a ____ is to a cook.

b. A catalog is to a shopper as a ____ is to one who dines.

c. A chemist is to a laboratory as a ____ is to a kitchen.

d. Woodworking tools are to a carpenter as ____ is to a butcher.

2. The omitted word is a homophone of the italicized word. Write the homophone.

to *desert* a ship　　　delicious ____

3. Write the list words that name these foods:

a. a vegetable　　　**b.** three desserts

4. Many English words have been borrowed from other languages. Using your dictionary, write the language from which each word below has been borrowed.

a. menu　　　**b.** chef

5. Which word has this respelling: (res′ ə pē)?

PROGRESS CHECK

WORD CHALLENGE

Some American-English words differ from British-English words. Write the American word that matches each British word listed below.

	British	*American*
a.	dessert	French fries
b.	maize	potato chips
c.	crisps	corn
d.	chips	fruit

REVIEW and EXTENSION 12

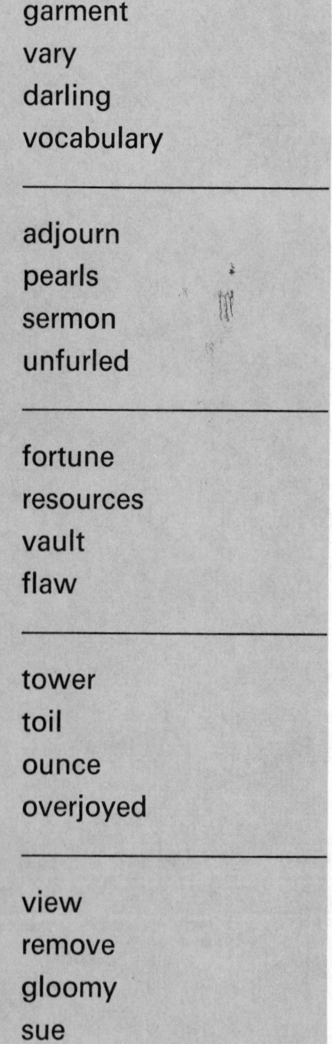
garment
vary
darling
vocabulary

adjourn
pearls
sermon
unfurled

fortune
resources
vault
flaw

tower
toil
ounce
overjoyed

view
remove
gloomy
sue

SOUNDS and PATTERNS

1. Say each word in the box. Notice that the different *r*-controlled vowel sounds are spelled with *ar*.

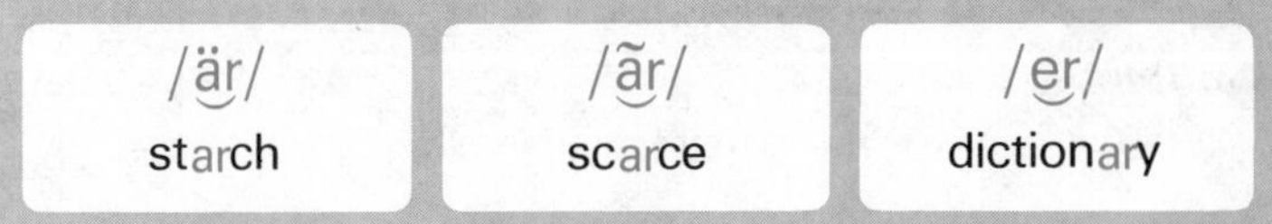

In which list words do you hear the sounds below?

a. /är/ **b.** /ãr/ **c.** /er/

2. Say the words below. Listen for /ėr/ and /ôr/.

a. Write list words in which you hear /ėr/.
b. Write list words in which you hear /ôr/.

3. In which list words do you hear /ô/, as in *dawn*?

4. Say the words below. Listen for the vowel sounds.

a. Write the list words in which you hear /ou/.
b. Write the list words in which you hear /oi/.

5. Say the words below. Listen for /ü/ and /yü/.

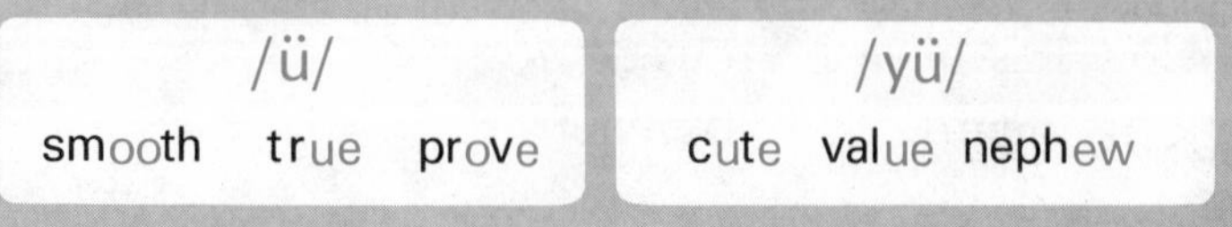

a. Write the list words in which you hear /ü/.
b. Write the list word in which you hear /yü/.

DICTIONARY

1. Write the words below in alphabetical order. Then check your list of words with the Spelling Dictionary.

furnish force fountain border fort
courage furnace fought

2. Study the dictionary entries at the right. Then write the word that completes the sentence.

An astronaut must have a great deal of training and ____.

3. Write each word below. After each, write the numeral that tells how many different meanings are given at the right for the entry.

a. review **b.** value

4. Write the word *urban*. Then write the antonym for *urban*.

5. Read the entry for *whom*. Write the abbreviation used to show that *whom* is a pronoun.

6. One of the words at the right is a plural form. Write the word. Then write the abbreviation that shows that this entry is the plural form of a noun.

7. Write the words that have these origins:

a. [From Latin *urbs* city]
b. [From Old French *cort* a court]
c. [From Latin *re* again + *videre* to see]

CHECK POINT

If you misspelled words in Units 7–11, decide why you made errors. Study those words again. Then study the new words.

cour age (kėr′ ij), *n.* Bravery. —*Ant.* **cowardice.** —**courageous,** *adj.* Full of courage; brave.

cour te ous (kėr′ tē əs), *adj.* Polite; having good manners. [From Old French *cort* a court.]

re gards (ri gärdz′), *n. pl.* Good wishes.

re view (ri vyü′), *v.* To look at or study again. [From Latin *re* again + *videre* to see.]

ur ban (ėr′ bən), *adj.* Of or having to do with a city or town, such as an *urban* center. [From Latin *urbs* city.] —*Ant.* **rural.**

val ue (val′ yü), *n.* Worth. —*v.* 1. To decide the worth in money. 2. To prize; to think highly of.

whom (hüm), *pron.* 1. What person? 2. Which person?

WORD STRUCTURE

1. Study the plural forms of base words ending with *y*.

Which list word is the plural form of *community?* of *courtesy?*

2. Study the base words and their *ing* forms in the box.

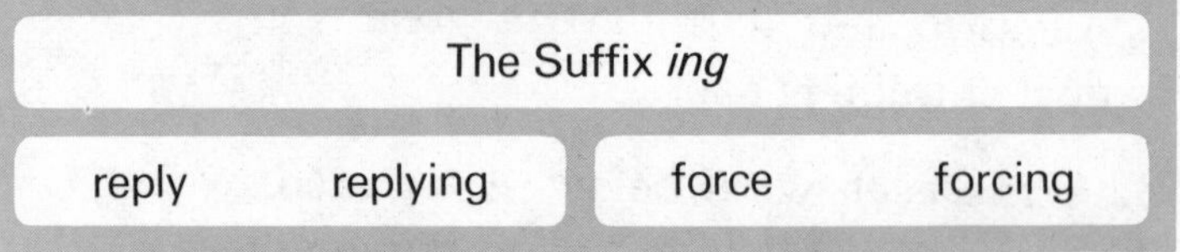

Write list words that are forms of these base words:

a. *excuse* **b.** *vary* **c.** *prove* **d.** *furnish*

3. A prefix and a suffix can be used with a base word.

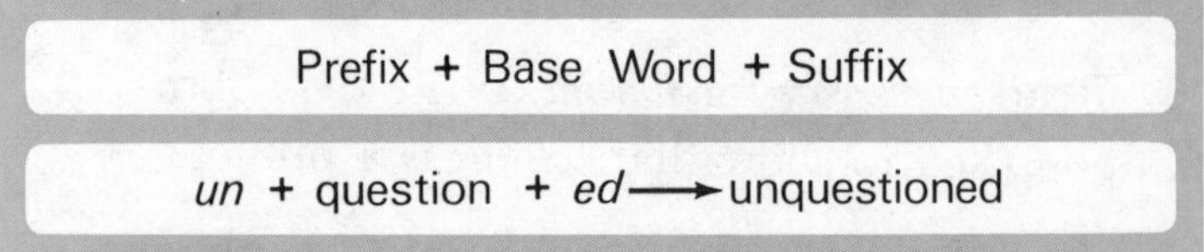

a. Write list words formed from the prefix *un* + a base word + the suffix *ed.*

b. Write the list words formed from *improve, nourish, adjourn.* Underline the suffix in each word.

4. Write list words to complete the following sentences. Underline the prefix or suffix in each word.

a. The sergeant received a ____ from army service.

b. We looked at the color slides through a ____.

c. My mother's ____ promoted her to a new job.

5. Compounds can be made by putting two words together. Write list words that are compounds.

courtesies
communities
furnishing
varying
proving
excusing
improvement
nourishment
unemployed
unsupported
adjournment
discharge
employer
viewer
overjoy
railway

PROGRESS CHECK

Be sure you can spell all the words in the first lists from Units 7–12.

court
poison
scarce
garment
furnish
toil
confuse
sue
mourn
cute
charge
bound
parents
shower
journal

ON YOUR OWN

1. Write the word from the lettered sentence that completes the sentence that follows it.

a. We must furnish the bedroom next year.
Can you ____ proof for your statement?

b. The charge for the merchandise was high.
Jim was in ____ of the class yesterday.

c. There was bound to be some confusion.
We ____ up the package.

2. Complete the puzzle with list words.

Across

1. harmful substance
4. clothing
6. house of law
8. to plead for

Down

1. mom and dad
2. rare
3. attractive, in a dainty way
5. to grieve
7. work

1			2					3
		4		5				
			6			7		
8								

torrent
arbor
poise
armor
cutlery
bombard

3. Write the word that belongs with each group.

a. raid, attack, ____ **b.** knives, forks, ____
c. grace, charm, ____ **d.** tree, garden, ____
e. downpour, flood, ____ **f.** knight, shield, ____

13

My sister is clever. She thinks of a new offer as an adventure into the future. No wonder she's a regular speaker at the factory union meetings.

offer
chapter
upper
member
timber
clever
grammar
motor
tractor
future
regular
factory
memory
adventure
manufacture
acre

SOUNDS and PATTERNS

1. Say the words in the box. Do you hear /ər/ in syllables that are stressed, or unstressed?

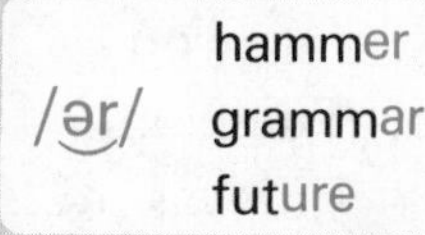

2. Write the letters that spell /ər/ in the word *hammer*, in the word *grammar*, and in the word *future*.

3. Write list words in which /ər/ is spelled:
a. *ar* **b.** *er* **c.** *re*

4. In which list words is /ər/ spelled with the letters *or*?

5. Which list word rhymes with *maker*? Underline the letters that spell /ər/.

In many words /ər/ is spelled *er, ar, or,* or *re*. Some words end with /ər/ spelled *re*.

6. The same word may be pronounced in two different ways. Which respelling fits your pronunciation of *factory*? Write **a** or **b**.
a. (fak′ tər ē) **b.** (fak′ trē)

Even though a word may be pronounced in different ways, its spelling may not change.

STRUCTURE and MEANING

1. Which list word is an antonym of each italicized word below?

a. *lower* floor **b.** *irregular* beat **c.** the *past*

2. Which list words have these Latin origins?

a. *movere,* meaning "to move"
b. *manus,* meaning "hand" + *facere,* meaning "to make"
c. *ad,* meaning "to" + *venire,* meaning "to come"

3. Answer the following questions. Then check your Spelling Dictionary.

a. Which list word comes from the French word *memoir*?
b. Which list word comes from the Latin word *membrum*?

4. ***DICTIONARY*** The underlined letters in *member* show a vowel-consonant-consonant-vowel letter pattern, or the **VCCV pattern.** Look at the syllabicated word. Between which two letters should *member* be divided?

member

mem ber

Words having the VCCV letter pattern are usually syllabicated between the two consonant letters.

5. Write the words below. Draw a curved line under the letters that spell each syllable.

a. chapter **b.** timber **c.** upper **d.** grammar

offer
chapter
upper
member
timber
clever
grammar
motor
tractor
future
regular
factory
memory
adventure
manufacture
acre

WORDS IN CODE

Use words from both lists.

6. The word *grammar* can be shown by this code: **ccvc′ cvc.** The code shows the order of the consonant and vowel letters in the word and the position of the stressed syllable.

Write the word that matches each coded word in the paragraph and that also fits the meaning clue.

The farmer's **ccvc′cvc** was broken. But the **cvc′cvc cvc** and **cvc′ v cvc** fixed it with a pair of **ccv′vcc.**

pliers
screwdriver
mortar
plaster
pattern
structure
janitor
carpenter
architecture

r r r
acre
regular

HANDWRITING Be sure to write the letter *r* carefully. It can be written in different ways, but it should not be confused with other letters. Practice writing *r*. Then write the words *acre* and *regular*.

pliers
screwdriver
mortar
plaster
pattern
structure
janitor
carpenter
architecture

CHECK POINT The doctor said it would be better to use less sugar. (K)

WORD KNOWLEDGE

1. Write two list words that complete each group of words below.

a. hammer, saw, ___, ___

b. cement, concrete, ___, ___

2. Shown below are the origins of two list words as given in a dictionary. Write the list words. Notice how each word has changed in meaning.

a. from Latin *carpentarius* (carriage maker) from *carpentum* (wagon)

b. from Latin *janitor* (door-keeper) from *janua* (door)

3. Write the list words that complete the following sentences.

The professional word for the designing of buildings is (a). The blueprint used is a kind of (b) for building a new (c).

WORD CHALLENGE

Each numeral in the illustration identifies an object named below. Match the numerals and the objects.

cornice
arch
column
keystone
capital

PROGRESS CHECK

14 The /ə/ Before /l/

The quarrel was about a bushel of apples that had been dumped into a barrel. This is the total story. What possible moral could there be?

SOUNDS and PATTERNS

1. Say each word in the box. Hear /əl/. See how /əl/ is spelled in each word. Do you hear /əl/ in a stressed, or in an unstressed, syllable in each word?

/əl/	simple
	shovel
	total

2. Copy the words from the box. Underline the letters that spell /əl/.

Many words end with /əl/. Three ways in which /əl/ may be spelled are *le, el, al*.

3. Write the list words in which /əl/ is spelled with the following letters.

a. *al* **b.** *el* **c.** *le*

4. Some sounds are spelled with two letters that are alike, such as *ll* in *roller*. These letters are called **double letters.** Write the list words that have double letters.

5. Write the list words in which /j/ is spelled with the letter g.

6. Write the list words for these respellings:

a. (ang′ kəl) **b.** (ang′ gəl)

7. Write the list word for this respelling: (kwôr′əl). Which letters spell /kw/?

simple
sample
angle
single
ankle
example
total
quarrel
angel
shovel
chapel
barrel
bushel
funeral
original
possible

simple
sample
angle
single
ankle
example
total
quarrel
angel
shovel
chapel
barrel
bushel
funeral
original
possible

STRUCTURE and MEANING

1. Write a list word that belongs with each set of words.

a. triple, double, ____ **b.** spade, hoe, ____
c. cathedral, church, ____ **d.** pint, quart, ____

2. The suffix *ly* added to a base word often makes a word that tells *how.* Write the *ly* forms of *total* and *original* to complete the sentence below.

We (a) planned to sing but are (b) unprepared today.

3. Notice the *ly* form of *gentle* in the box.

a. Which letter in *gentle* is not in *gently?*
b. Which letter in *gently* is not in *gentle?*

gentle
gently

4. Write the *ly* form of *simple* or *possible* for each blank.

a. The stage was ____ decorated.
b. We can't ____ be there an hour early.

5. Write *angels* or *angles* to complete this sentence:

We made a square by holding rulers at right ____.

6. ***DICTIONARY*** Study the syllabication of the words in the box. The last syllable of a word ending with *le* usually begins with the consonant letter just before *le.*

Write each word below. Draw a curved line under the letters that spell each syllable.

a. ankle **b.** simple **c.** possible

tinsel
carol
casual
crystal
icicle
pedal
mantel
mantle
peddle

SIMILES

Use words from both lists.

7. An imaginative comparison of two unlike things, using the word *like* or *as,* is called a **simile.** Complete each simile with a list word.

a. The water is as clear as ____.
b. The baby behaved like an ____.
c. Jay's hands were as cold as an ____.
d. The snow glittered like ____.

HANDWRITING The letters *e* and *l* are looped letters. Practice writing *el, le,* and *al.* Be sure *el* and *al* look different. Make *l* tall. Then practice writing the words, *angel, angle,* and *total.*

el le al

angel angle

total

CHECK POINT It seems that several people have been having trouble with that model car. L

tinsel
carol
casual
crystal
icicle
pedal
mantel
mantle
peddle

WORD KNOWLEDGE

1. Write pairs of homophones for each sentence.

a. A lever operated by foot is a ___, but to sell in small amounts, often from door to door, is to ___.

b. The shelf above the fireplace is a ___, but a covering or a long coat is a ___.

2. Which list words complete the story?

It's Christmas. From each rooftop hangs an (a), which looks like (b). The children have strung (c) on the tree and are out singing a (d) or two. They are dressed in (e) clothes.

PROGRESS CHECK

WORD CHALLENGE

New Year greetings are shown below in four languages. Write the name of each language. Use an encyclopedia if you need help. Look under *New Year's Day.*

a. Shana Tova
b. Buon Capo d'Anno
c. Feliz Año Nuevo
d. Gutes Neues Jahr

15

Imagine our surprise when we won tickets to a science-fiction convention. My favorite exhibit was opposite the exit. We could walk inside a flying saucer.

tablet
ticket
bucket
spirit
exhibit
private
accurate
sudden
heaven
citizen
religion
convention
medicine
imagine
favorite
opposite

SOUNDS and PATTERNS

1. Each picture below suggests a list word. A clue to each word is under the picture. Say each word. The last two sounds in each word are /i/ and /t/. Is the /it/ in a stressed, or in an unstressed, syllable?

2. Write the word for each picture. Underline the words in which /it/ is spelled in the VC*e* pattern.

> The /it/in a final unstressed syllable may be spelled *et, it, ate,* or *ite.*

3. Write the list words in which final /it/ is spelled with these letters:

a. *it* **b.** *ite* **c.** *et* **d.** *ate*

4. Say each word in the box. Notice the letters that spell /ən/. Write the list words in which /ən/ is spelled:

/ən/	oven engine nation

a. *ine* **b.** *en* **c.** *on*

STRUCTURE and MEANING

1. Write the list word that is a synonym of each word below.
   a. display **b.** pretend **c.** correct

2. Find *favor* in the Spelling Dictionary. Notice the other forms shown after the meaning. These are **derived forms** of *favor*. Write a form of *favor* for each blank in the sentence.
   Their (a) candidate received a (b) vote.

> A word form that is a different part of speech from its base word is a derived form.

3. Write the list word that is a derived form of *convene.*

4. The suffix *tion* or *ation* is often used with a base word. Write the derived form of *imagine* that fits the meaning of the sentence below. Underline the suffix.
   Maria's painting shows much ____.

5. ***DICTIONARY*** Study the dictionary entry at the right. Then answer these questions:

   sud den (sud′ ən), *adj.* 1. Not expected. 2. Quick. **—suddenly,** *adv.* In a quick way. **—suddenness,** *n.* Quickness.

   a. What part of speech is *sudden*?
   b. Which derived form of *sudden* completes each sentence?
   Karen was surprised by the ____ of the storm.
   The black clouds had appeared quite ____.

tablet
ticket
bucket
spirit
exhibit
private
accurate
sudden
heaven
citizen
religion
convention
medicine
imagine
favorite
opposite

WORD ORIGINS

Use words from both lists.

6. Write words that have the Latin origins below.
   a. *com,* meaning "together," + *venire,* meaning "to come"
   b. *inter,* meaning "between," + *mittere,* meaning "to send"
   c. *dis,* meaning "out," + *metiri,* meaning "to measure"

stadium
siren
champion
cushion
intermission
dimension
coliseum
tournament
festival

b f h k l
tablet
exhibit

HANDWRITING Are you forming upward loop letters carefully? Practice writing the letters *b, f, h, k, l.* Then write *tablet* and *exhibit*. Now practice writing other list words that contain these letters.

stadium
siren
champion
cushion
intermission
dimension
coliseum
tournament
festival

CHECK POINT The women listened as my friend told which market sold berries. M

WORD KNOWLEDGE

1. Write the two list words that mean a large structure with seats for people who watch games or sports.

2. Complete the paragraph with list words.

Each New Year's Day two football teams compete in the Rose Bowl. Each team is a (a) team of its conference. Before the game, there is a big celebration, or (b). Because people compete for the best float in the parade, it is called a (c).

3. Which word completes each group of words?

a. whistle, horn, ____

b. pause, recess, ____

4. Answer the following questions.

a. Which word means "extent of measurement"?

b. Which word names something soft?

PROGRESS CHECK

WORD CHALLENGE

In ancient or medieval times people watched performances at the places named below. Tell what kind of performance they saw in each place. You may use a dictionary or an encyclopedia.

a. odeum **b.** amphitheater
c. tiltyard **d.** hippodrome
e. campus **f.** palaestra

16 Unstressed Syllables

WITH POTHOLES
The dangerous surface of the street is a menace. The people are nervous. In fact, they are furious. But the city has promised courteous service.

SOUNDS and PATTERNS

1. Say each word in the mobile. The last vowel sound in each word is /i/.

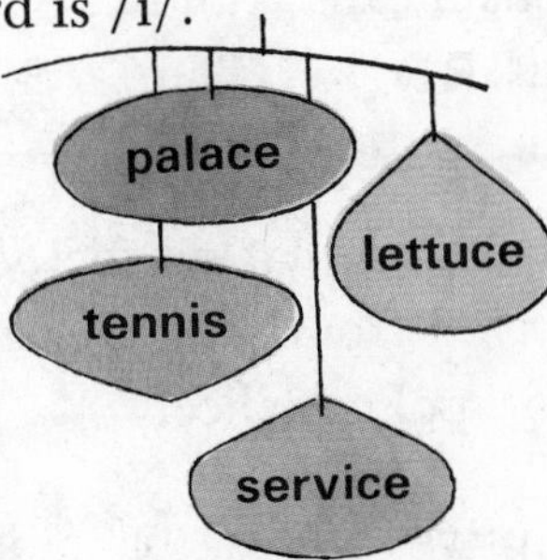

a. Write each of the words. Underline the letter that spells /i/ in each word.

b. Is the /i/ in a stressed, or in an unstressed, syllable?

When the /i/ is followed by /s/ in an unstressed syllable, the /is/ may be spelled in the VC*e* pattern: *ace, ice, ise, uce.* Sometimes /is/ is spelled with *is.*

2. Write list words in which /is/ is spelled:

a. in the VC*e* pattern

b. with the letters *is*

3. Write the list words derived from the base words *nerve* and *courage.* Underline the letters in each word that spell /əs/.

4. Write the other list words in which /əs/ is spelled with the letters *ous.*

The most common way of spelling final /əs/ is with the letters *ous.*

palace
surface
menace
practice
justice
service
nervous
lettuce
promise
tennis
furious
dangerous
religious
courageous
courteous
iris

palace
surface
menace
practice
justice
service
nervous
lettuce
promise
tennis
furious
dangerous
religious
courageous
courteous
iris

STRUCTURE and MEANING

1. The word *slices* has two units of meaning. The base word *slice* means "a thin piece cut from something." The suffix *s* means "plural." Study the units of meaning in the box.

slice + plural ⟶ slices

Write each word for the units of meaning below.

a. *promise* + plural ⟶ ? **b.** *palace* + plural ⟶ ?

2. The suffix *ous* means "full of." Write the *ous* forms of the following words.

a. danger **b.** fury **c.** nerve

3. Write a list word that correctly completes each phrase and that is derived from the word in parentheses.

a. (courage) police officer **b.** (religion) service

Some descriptive words, or adjectives, are formed by adding the suffix *ous* to a base word. Some *ous* forms do not contain all the letters of the base word.

4. Which list word can be used in each of these sentences?

a. Maria was in the ____ of her country for two years.

b. The submarine will appear on the ____ in a few minutes.

sponges
fungus
species
porous
apparatus
octopus
amphibians
crustaceans
mollusks

5. Write the word that names the colored part of the eye.

6. ***DICTIONARY*** In your Spelling Dictionary, find the language from which the word *courteous* is derived. Then write the meaning of the word from which *courteous* came.

NONSENSE RHYMES Use words from both lists.

7. Write a word that completes each rhyme.

a. A house in Dallas seems like a ____.

b. At playing tennis, I'm a ____.

c. The diver plunges for the ____.

HANDWRITING Compare the small *s* with the capital S. Practice writing *s* and S. Be sure to close small *s* at the line. Practice writing *service* and *promise*. Then write: Sponges have a rough surface.

s S s S
service
promise

CHECK POINT I notice that there are various furnaces on sale all through February. Ⓜ

sponges
fungus
species
porous
apparatus
octopus
amphibians
crustaceans
mollusks

WORD KNOWLEDGE

1. Complete each blank in the paragraph with a different list word.

A sponge is a sea animal. The picture shows two kinds, or (a), of (b). Many tiny holes make the sponge very (c).

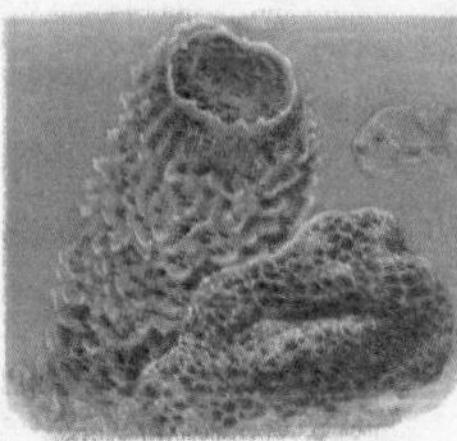

2. Write words that have the meanings below.

a. a plant that lives on other living things
b. equipment used for a special purpose

3. Which word comes from the Greek *amphibios,* meaning "leading a double life"? This word names animals that can live either on land or in water, such as frogs.

4. Write list words that have these origins:

a. Latin *crusta,* meaning "shell"
b. Latin *molluscus,* meaning "soft"
c. Greek *okta,* meaning "eight," and *pous,* meaning "foot"

PROGRESS CHECK

WORD CHALLENGE

Write the words *crustaceans* and *mollusks* as column headings. Write the names of the animals below under the correct headings.

lobster	*crab*	*octopus*
snail	*shrimp*	*crayfish*
oyster	*scallop*	*clam*

17

The student sat and gazed
Into the distance.
How soon could he get a license
And experience the thrills
Of driving over distant hills?

student
current
agent
excellent
consonant
ignorant
balance
importance
distant
distance
different
difference
absent
absence
experience
license

SOUNDS and PATTERNS

1. Say each word in the box. Listen for /ənt/ in the final syllable.

/ənt/	student distant

a. Do you hear /ənt/ in a stressed syllable, or in an unstressed, syllable?

b. Write each word. Underline the letters that spell /ənt/.

2. Write the words in which /ənt/ is spelled:

a. with *ant* **b.** with *ent*

The /ənt/ in a final unstressed syllable is spelled with the letters *ent* or *ant*.

3. Say each word in the box below. Listen for /əns/. Write each word. Underline the four letters in each word that spell /əns/.

/əns/	balance	absence	license

4. In which other list words is /əns/ spelled

a. as in *balance*? **b.** as in *absence*?

The /əns/ in a final unstressed syllable is spelled in three ways: *ance, ence,* or *ense.*

STRUCTURE and MEANING

1. Write the following list words. Draw a curved line under the letters that spell each syllable. Beside each word, write the number of syllables in the word.

a. ignorant **b.** excellent **c.** importance
d. different **e.** consonant **f.** experience

2. Write the correct form of *differ* for each sentence below. Underline the suffix in each word.

a. The bottles hold ____ amounts.
b. The ____ between them is one pint.

3. Write list words for each pair of respellings below. Underline the letter in each word that spells /ə/.

a. (ab′ sənt), (ab′ səns) **b.** (dis′ tənt), (dis′ təns)

Many words ending with the letters *ent* have related forms ending with *ence*. Many words ending with *ant* have related forms ending with *ance*.

4. Write list words that come from these Latin words:

a. *currere* (to run) **b.** *licere* (be allowed)

5. ***DICTIONARY*** Find the word *balance* in your dictionary.

a. Which two parts of speech are shown for *balance*?
b. Two other forms of *balance* are shown in your dictionary. Write the correct form of *balance* for each sentence. Angela is ____ herself on a rope. William ____ himself for thirty seconds.

student.
current
agent
excellent
consonant
ignorant
balance
importance
distant
distance
different
difference
absent
absence
experience
license

PROOFREADING Use words from both lists.

6. Some words below are incomplete. Rewrite each word, adding the correct letters.

a. The odometer is an instrum__ that measures dist__.
b. Are you ignor__ about pollution in the environm__?
c. The stud__ had excell__ results with his studies.

violent
experiment
elements
abundant
fragment
instrument
environment
continent
inhabitant

entantment
student
importance

HANDWRITING Write the letters *e, a, n,* and *m* carefully. Be sure your writing is legible when you connect the letter *e* or *a* to *n.* Practice writing *ent, ant,* and *ment.* Then write the words *student* and *importance.*

violent
experiment
elements
abundant
fragment
instrument
environment
continent
inhabitant

WORD CHALLENGE

The word *ecology* means the study of living things in relation to their environment and to each other. Which of the following subjects would an ecologist be likely to study?

conservation	*counterpoint*
water pollution	*population*
solar energy	*semantics*
oratorio	*organisms*

CHECK POINT In every sentence, they used very poor grammar. O

WORD KNOWLEDGE

1. Use a list word to complete each sentence.

Puerto Rico is not far from the (a) of South America. Usually the natural (b) is very pleasant, but sometimes the (c) can get (d). This picture shows an (e) who just heard of hurricane warnings.

2. Which list word is an antonym of
a. scarce? **b.** whole? **c.** calm?

3. Complete each sentence with a list word.
a. Clara plays a musical ____.
b. Let's ____ with several brands of soup.

PROGRESS CHECK

18 REVIEW and EXTENSION

bother
signature
vapor
lunar

comical
panel
dimple
stable

brackets
bandits
warden
attraction

tremendous
crevice
terrace
basis

instant
instance
dependent
dependence

SOUNDS and PATTERNS

1. The /ə/ plus a consonant in an unstressed syllable is spelled in different ways. Notice the letters that spell each sound.

/ər/		/əl/	/ən/
chapter	motor	sample	sudden
grammar	future	total	attention
		shovel	imagine

In which list words do you hear the following sounds? Underline the letters that spell the sounds.

a. /ər/ **b.** /ən/ **c.** /əl/

2. Say the words below. Hear /is/ and /əs/.

/is/		/əs/
promise	surface	dangerous
tennis	practice	religious

a. Write two new list words in which /is/ is spelled in the VC*e* pattern.
b. In which list word is /is/ spelled *is*?
c. Which list word has /əs/ spelled *ous*?

3. Write the words *tickets, spirits, favorites.* Underline the letters of the unstressed syllable in each word. Then write two list words in which you hear the same unstressed syllable.

4. Write the list words in which you hear the sounds below. Underline the letters that spell the sounds.

a. /əns/ **b.** /ənt/

5. In which list words is a single consonant sound spelled with double letters?

clev er (klev′ ər), *adj.* Skillful; intelligent. —**cleverness,** *n.* Being clever; showing intelligence. —**cleverly,** *adv.* In a clever way.

fac to ry (fak′ tər ē, fak′ trē), *n., pl.* **factories.** A manufacturing plant; a building in which things are made. [From Latin *facere* to make.]

li cense (lī′ səns), *n.* A right granted by law; a paper showing a specific right a person has earned. [From Latin *licere* to be permitted.]

mem o ry (mem′ ər ē, mem′ rē), *n., pl.* **memories.** The ability to remember; what one remembers.

nerv ous (nėr′ vəs), *adj.* 1. Having to do with nerves. 2. Being easily excited; not calm. —**nervousness,** *n.* Anxiety.

prac tice (prak′ tis), *n.* 1. Action done many times over for skill. 2. The business of a lawyer or doctor. —*v.,* **practicing, practiced.** To work at; to do regularly. —*Syn.* **drill; exercise.**

sta ble[1] (stā′ bəl), *n.* A building in which horses are kept. —*v.* To put or keep in a stable. [From Latin *stabulum* a standing place.]

sta ble[2] (stā′ bəl), *adj.* 1. Firmly established; not likely to change suddenly. 2. Steady in purpose; firm. 3. Lasting; enduring. [From Latin *stabilis* able to stand.]

DICTIONARY

1. Read the entry for *practice* at the left.

a. What other forms of *practice* are shown?

b. Write the synonyms shown in the entry.

2. Complete the sentence with the correct derived form of *clever* shown in the entry.

He very ____ hid his embarrassment.

3. A doctor must have a license to practice medicine. Read the entry for *license* at the left. Write the meaning of the Latin word *licere,* from which *license* is derived.

4. Notice the entry for *memory.* Two pronunciations are shown. Write *2* or *3* to show the number of syllables you pronounce in *memory.*

5. Two pronunciations are given for another word at the left. Write the word.

6. Notice the syllables for the entry *nervous.* The entry word shows where to divide the word at the end of a line of writing. The respelling shows where to divide the word when you pronounce it. After which letter in *nervous* would you place a hyphen at the end of a writing line?

7. Read both entries for the word *stable.* Write *1* or *2* to show which entry has this origin:

[From Latin *stabilis* able to stand.]

CHECK POINT

If you misspelled words in Units 13–17, decide why you made errors. Study those words again. Then study the new words.

WORD STRUCTURE

1. Study the way a derived form of a word is made from a base word. Sometimes the final letter of the base word is omitted or changed when the suffix is added.

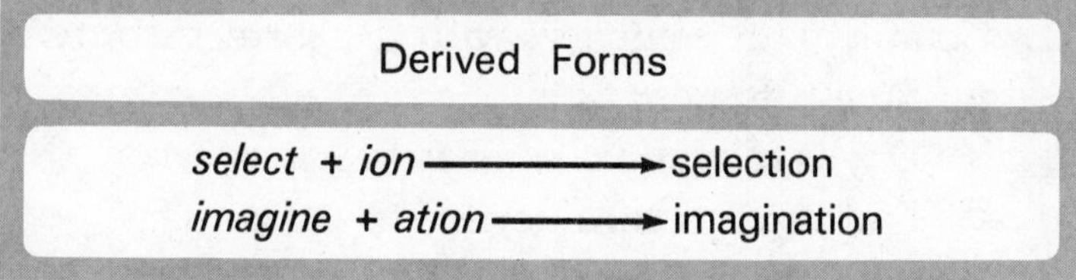

Derived Forms
select + *ion* → selection
imagine + *ation* → imagination

Write the list word that is a derived form of the word in parentheses in each phrase below.

a. (confuse) in the halls   **b.** (observe) of waste
c. (vary) from routine   **d.** art (exhibit)

2. Study the derived forms of words below.

famous	famously	courage	courageous

a. Write the derived forms that have the *ly* suffix. Underline the base words.
b. Which list word is a derived form of *poison*? of *desire*? Underline the suffix in each word.
c. Which letter was dropped from *desire* before the suffix *ous* was added?

3. Compare the vowel letters in the unstressed syllable of each pair of words below.

distant, distance	absent, absence

Write the list words that end with /ənt/. After each word, write its /əns/ form.

confusion
exhibition
observation
variation
regularly
privately
instantly
poisonous
desirous
excellent
excellence
ignorant
ignorance
important
importance

sudden
original
student
private
ignorant
different
offer
angel
upper
courageous
tennis
justice
chapter
absent
motor
courteous

PROGRESS CHECK

Be sure you can spell all the words in the first lists from Units 13–18.

ON YOUR OWN

1. Complete the sentences with the correct words.

- **a.** Rich is to poor as public is to ____.
- **b.** Day is to night as same is to ____.
- **c.** Evil is to good as devil is to ____.

2. Complete the puzzle with list words.

Across

1. one who studies
5. knowing nothing
6. propose something
7. higher

Down

2. a game
3. section of a book
4. an engine

3. Write an antonym for each word.

a. cowardly **b.** unfairness **c.** present
d. gradual **e.** impolite **f.** copy

carpenter
pattern
screwdriver
abundant
fragment
pliers
structure
porous

4. Answer the following questions.

- **a.** Which word means "plenty of"?
- **b.** Which word means "a model"?
- **c.** Which word means "full of tiny holes"?

5. Can you decode the sentence below? Each letter stands for the letter that precedes it in the alphabet: *b* stands for *a; c,* for *b*, etc. Write each italicized word

B *dbsqfoufs* pgufo vtft b *tdsfxesjwfs* boe
qmjfst up sfqbjs b *gsbhnfou* pg b *tusvduvsf.*

19 The Consonant /k/

Let's hear an extra chorus
For the folks who didn't quit.
An orchestra we'll never lack—
The public saw to it!

SOUNDS and PATTERNS

1. Say the words in the box. Listen for the consonant /k/.

a. In which words do you hear final /k/? Underline the letters that spell /k/.

b. Which words begin with /k/? Underline the letters that spell /k/.

/k/
rock
public
keen
chorus

2. Write the other list words in which /k/ is spelled as in the words below.

a. rock **b.** public **c.** chorus

3. In which word is /k/ spelled with double letters? Underline the double letters.

The /k/ may be spelled *k, c, ck,* or *ch*.

4. Write the word for this respelling: (kwit). Which letters spell /kw/?

5. In which other list words is /kw/ spelled as in the word *quit*?

The /kw/ is spelled with the letters *qu*.

6. Write the words in which /ks/ is spelled:

a. with *x* **b.** with *ks*

keen
public
attic
account
lack
rock
chorus
orchestra
stomach
ache
chord
quit
banquet
acquainted
extra
folks

keen
public
attic
account
lack
rock
chorus
orchestra
stomach
ache
chord
quit
banquet
acquainted
extra
folks

STRUCTURE and MEANING

1. Which word can be a synonym for each word below?
a. spare **b.** sharp **c.** resign **d.** report **e.** feast

2. Which list word is a past-tense form? Underline the past-tense suffix. Write the past-tense form of *lack*.

3. When a word ends with *s*, you usually add *es* to form the plural. Write the plural form of *chorus*.

4. Write *quit* and *quite* to complete the sentence below.
Kim is ___ happy with her job and doesn't plan to ___.

5. Write the two list words that complete the sentence.
The school ___ sang the wrong ___.

6. Which word can be used to complete the sentences?
James must ___ for his time. He has a bank ___.

7. ***DICTIONARY*** Study these keys to words that begin with /k/. They can help you find words in the dictionary that begin with the letters *k* and *c*.

> The /k/ at the beginning of a word is often spelled with *c*. When a word begins with /k/ followed by /e/, /ē/, /i/, or /ī/, the /k/ is usually spelled with *k*.
>
> came — cold kept — kite

Write the letter that spells initial /k/ in each case.
a. _erosene **b.** _arnival **c.** _ind **d.** _olumn

choral
choir
network
quartet
sextet
octet
balcony
comedy
acoustics

PROOFREADING Use words from both lists.

8. The blanks show that one or two letters are missing from each word. Rewrite each word correctly.
The producer la_s funds to improve the a_ousti_s in the auditorium. So the or_estra and _oir have quit.

HANDWRITING Compare the letters g and *q*. Both letters begin the same way. Notice that the lower loop of *q* is at the right of the slanted downward stroke. Practice writing g, *q*, and *qu*. Now write *quit* and *banquet*.

g q qu

quit

banquet

CHECK POINT Pack the box of Christmas cookies quickly, but be sure not to break any. **P**

choral
choir
network
quartet
sextet
octet
balcony
comedy
acoustics

WORD KNOWLEDGE

1. Write words that mean a group of instruments or singers composed of the following numbers.

a. four **b.** eight **c.** six

2. Complete the paragraph with list words.

The (a) was singing on a TV (b). The viewing public sat in the theater (c), where the (d) were perfect.

3. Which list word is a homophone of *coral*?

4. Which word is an antonym of *tragedy*?

PROGRESS CHECK

WORD CHALLENGE

One or more letters are missing in each word below. The symbol shows the sound of the missing letter or letters. Write each word correctly. Check the dictionary if necessary.

/k/ __ara__ter	/k/ __aos
/k/ __oda__	/k/ __arisma
/k/ __ameo	/s/ __ipher
/k/ iambi__	/s/ __upple

20

It was difficult to go forward,
The crowd was getting rough.
We couldn't use a telephone
Or even find a megaphone.
We'd sit. We'd had enough!

wolf
loaf
golf
yourself
forward
afterward
certificate
suffer
traffic
difficult
coffee
physical
telephone
telegraph
rough
enough

SOUNDS and PATTERNS

1. Say *loaf, wolf,* and *golf.*

- **a.** Write each word.
- **b.** Do you hear /f/ at the end of each word?

2. Which two final letters are common to *wolf* and *golf?* Do you hear both sounds?

3. In which other list word do you hear the same final sounds as in *wolf* and *golf?*

4. In which words do you hear /f/ in these sentences? Underline the letters that spell /f/.

- **a.** Heavy traffic made driving difficult.
- **b.** Afterward she received her certificate.

The /f/ may be spelled with *f* or *ff*.

5. Which word begins with /f/ spelled by **a.** a single *f?* **b.** two different letters?

6. In which list words do you hear /f/ in this sentence? Underline the letters that spell /f/.
The doctor told Mother on the telephone that she might suffer from drinking coffee.

7. Write *telegraph, rough,* and *enough.* Underline the letters that spell /f/.

Sometimes /f/ is spelled with the letters *ph* or *gh*.

STRUCTURE and MEANING

wolf
loaf
golf
yourself
forward
afterward
certificate
suffer
traffic
difficult
coffee
physical
telephone
telegraph
rough
enough

1. Write the list word that is an antonym of each word below.

a. backward **b.** easy **c.** smooth

2. Write the list words that have the same suffix. Underline the suffix in each word. Then tell what the suffix means. Use your Spelling Dictionary.

3. Write list words that mean the same as the italicized phrases in the sentences below.

a. No one likes to *feel hardship or pain.*

b. This *official paper* will prove your birth date and name.

4. The prefix *tele* comes from the Greek and means "far off" or "at a distance." Write the list words that come from the prefix *tele* and these Greek words:

a. *graphein,* meaning "to write"

b. *phone,* meaning "sound"

5. ***DICTIONARY*** An irregular plural spelling usually follows an entry word. Use the dictionary to answer the questions.

a. What is the plural spelling of *wolf, loaf, yourself?*

b. Which letters correctly complete the statement below?

The plural form of a singular word ending with *f* is usually spelled by changing — to — and adding —.

JUST FOR FUN Use words from both lists.

welfare
sheriff
feverish
specific
terrific
sufficient
pharynx
transfusion
infirmary

6. Have you ever seen *laugh* spelled *lauf,* or *phrase* spelled *frase?* Probably not, but these strange spellings would be correct if /f/ were always spelled with the letter *f*.

Change each strange spelling below to a list word. Here are two clues: The letters are scrambled, and the letter *f* has been substituted for *ph* or *gh* representing /f/.

a. lacisyf **b.** enoflete **c.** ourf

d. fargelet **e.** fuone **f.** nxyraf

traffic
telephone
rough

HANDWRITING All letters should slant in the same direction. Letters that loop above and below the line give a clue to the slant of letters. Practice writing *traffic, telephone,* and *rough.*

welfare
sheriff
feverish
specific
terrific
sufficient
pharynx
transfusion
infirmary

CHECK POINT I can't hear half of what is said in class because you cough so much. (F)

WORD KNOWLEDGE

1. Which word belongs with each group of words?

a. police officer, detective, ____
b. larynx, esophagus, ____
c. hospital, clinic, ____

2. Which list word is a synonym of

a. enough? **b.** exact?

3. A person who says, "I fared well on my trip," means that things went well.

a. Which list word is a compound derived from the words *well* and *fare?*
b. Which letter in *well* is omitted in the compound?

4. Write a list word to complete this sentence: Emilio required a blood ____.

5. What does the prefix *trans* mean in the word *transfusion?*

6. Which list word is a form of each of the following words?

a. fever **b.** specify **c.** terrify

PROGRESS CHECK

WORD CHALLENGE

Many medical terms used today come from these Greek words: *otos* (ear), *psyche* (the mind), *dermatos* (skin), *ophthalmos* (eye), *podos* (foot).

Using the clues above, tell what each of these doctors treats: *dermatologist, psychiatrist, podiatrist, otologist, ophthalmologist.*

21 The Consonants /j/ and /g/

Is knowledge equally available
To the prisoner in jail,
To the soldier with a magazine,
To the engineer creating energy,
And to the student in college?

SOUNDS and PATTERNS

1. Write the list words that begin with /j/.

2. In which list words is /j/ spelled g, *ge*, or *dge*? Check (✓) the word that ends with *dge*.

> The /j/ is usually spelled with *j* or g. At the ends of words, /j/ is spelled with *ge* or *dge*.

3. Say each word in the box. Listen for /g/, as in *get*.
Write each word. Underline the letters that spell /g/.

governor	magazine	guide	league

> The /g/ may be spelled with g, *gu*, or *gue*. Usually when /g/ is spelled with g, the vowel letter *a*, *o*, or *u* follows the g.

4. Write another list word in which /g/ is spelled as in *league*.

5. In which list word is gg used to spell both the /g/ and /j/? Draw a line under the g that spells /j/.

6. Write the word in which /j/ is spelled *di*.

jail
jury
arrange
advantage
college
knowledge
vegetables
energy
engineer
suggest
governor
magazine
guide
league
catalogue
soldier

jail
jury
arrange
advantage
college
knowledge
vegetables
energy
engineer
suggest
governor
magazine
guide
league
catalogue
soldier

STRUCTURE and MEANING

1. Complete the following comparisons with list words.

a. A mayor is to a city as a ____ is to a state.
b. A pilot is to an airplane as an ____ is to a train.
c. A cage is to an animal as a ____ is to a criminal.

2. Write the list word that can be used in both of the following sentences.

My sister plans to join a bowling ____.
The weary traveler had another ____ to go before he reached town.

3. Write the plural form of each of the following words.

a. college **b.** advantage **c.** guide **d.** jury

4. Write each word below and draw a curved line under the letters that spell each syllable.

a. advantage **b.** governor **c.** vegetables

5. ***DICTIONARY*** Some words can be spelled in more than one way. In some dictionaries, the alternate spelling immediately follows the entry word. In others, it is found at the very end of the definition.

a. Find *catalogue* in your Spelling Dictionary. Write the alternate spelling of this word.
b. Write the alternate spelling of *jail*. Then tell what group of people use this spelling.

gems
jewels
jade
jasper
agate
garnet
nugget
graphite
mineralogy

COMPLETING WORD GROUPS Use words from both lists.

6. Complete each group of words below with a form of a list word. You will need different suffixes with the list words.

a. sailors, marines, ____
b. journals, pamphlets, ____
c. hint, proposal, ____
d. active, vigorous, ____
e. geologist, biologist, ____
f. favorable, beneficial, ____

HANDWRITING The letter g starts like *a*. The letter *j* starts like *i*. Both downward loops of g and *j* slant in the same direction. They extend one half space below the line. Practice writing *jury* and *suggest*.

g j
jury
suggest

CHECK POINT I guess the two girls will just go across the village bridge. Q

gems
jewels
jade
jasper
agate
garnet
nugget
graphite
mineralogy

WORD KNOWLEDGE

1. Write the list word that names the study of the science of minerals.

2. Which two words classify precious stones?

3. Some people collect gems as a hobby. They may cut various varieties of quartz, which they find in rocks. These stones can be polished and used to make jewelry.

Which list words name stones used to make ornaments and jewelry?

4. Which word names a lump of native gold?

5. Which word names the lead used in pencils?

6. Which word names the gems used in the works of a watch?

PROGRESS CHECK

WORD CHALLENGE

Find the meaning of *birthstone* in an encyclopedia or dictionary.

a. Make a list of the birthstones for every month of the year.

b. Tell what your birthstone is and its symbolic meaning.

amethyst

22

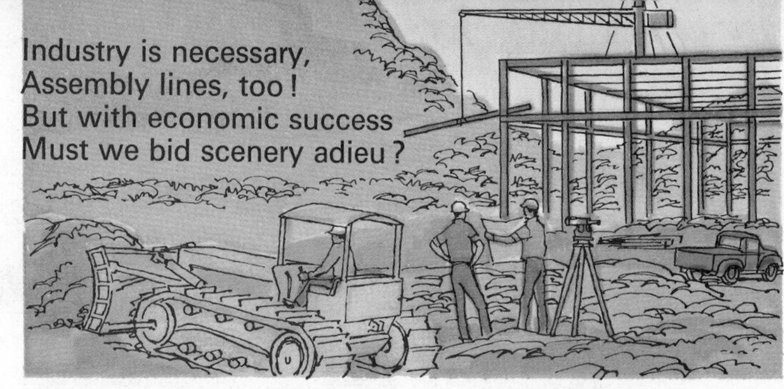
Industry is necessary,
Assembly lines, too!
But with economic success
Must we bid scenery adieu?

semester
satisfactory
thus
else
minister
press
congress
assembly
success
scenery
cement
civil
cycle
sincerely
necessary
industry

SOUNDS and PATTERNS

1. The words in the box begin with /s/. Write each word. Underline the letters that spell /s/ at the beginning of the words. Check (✓) the word in which /s/ is spelled with two letters.

/s/	semester civil scenery

2. Which other list words begin with /s/?

3. Look again at the words in which /s/ is spelled with the letter *c*. Then write the letters that complete this statement:

When /s/ is spelled with *c*, the *c* may be followed by the letter —, —, or —.

4. Which list words end with /s/? Underline the letters that spell final /s/.

> The /s/ may be spelled with *s, ss, c, sc*, or *s* followed by *e*.

5. The words below can be completed by letters that spell /s/. Write each word correctly. Underline the letters that spell /s/.

a. indu__try **b.** mini__ter
c. ne__e__ary **d.** a__embly
e. __in__erely **f.** __eme__ter

6. Write the list word in which *cc* spells two different sounds.

STRUCTURE and MEANING

1. Which list word comes from *sincere*? from *scene*?

2. Write a list word for each meaning below. Beside the word, write the number of syllables in the word.

   a. business **b.** good enough **c.** achievement
   d. landscape **e.** essential **f.** part of a school term

3. Write the correct forms of *satisfy* and *assembly* for this sentence:

   We were ___ with both school ___.

4. Write words that correctly complete these sentences:

   a. The seasons of the year make a ___ of time.
   b. The commission is studying the ___ defense program.

5. ***DICTIONARY*** Find *press* in your Spelling Dictionary and read its meanings. Write the letter of each sentence below. After each letter, write the number of the dictionary meaning that matches the meaning of *press* in the sentence.

   a. Our mayor held a conference with the press.
   b. A press keeps a tennis racket from warping.

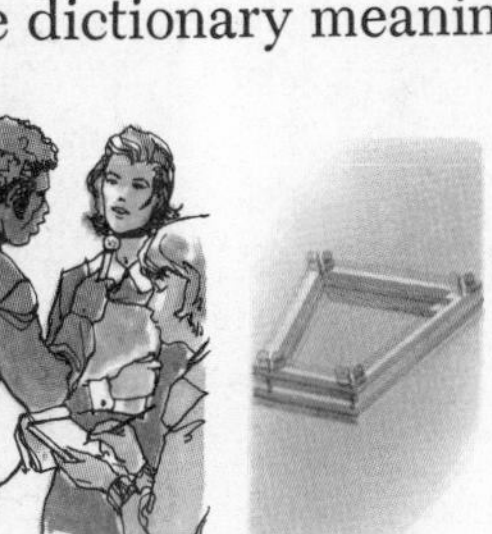

semester
satisfactory
thus
else
minister
press
congress
assembly
success
scenery
cement
civil
cycle
sincerely
necessary
industry

SYLLABIC CODES

Use words from both lists.

6. The syllabic code for *assembly* can be shown this way: — —′ —. This code shows that *assembly* has three syllables and that the second syllable is stressed.

Write words that complete the paragraph below. Each word must fit both the syllabic code and the meaning clues.

Officials from the steel —′ — — set a — —′ time to meet. The discussion concerned the new building site. They — —′ — hoped the construction would not spoil the —′ — — for a —′ — — of several miles.

sphere
hemisphere
axis
radius
cylinder
circumference
precise
bisects
circular

success
sincerely
necessary

HANDWRITING For legible writing, keep even spaces between letters. Do not crowd letters. Do not put too much space between letters. Practice writing the words *success, sincerely*, and *necessary*.

sphere
hemisphere
axis
radius
cylinder
circumference
precise
bisects
circular

CHECK POINT Since I took science classes instead, I can't answer questions about art. Ⓡ

WORD KNOWLEDGE

Use a list word to complete each statement about the figures below.

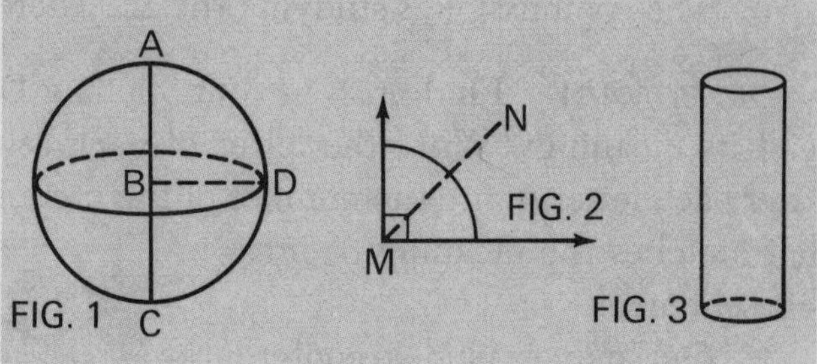

1. Figure 1 is a model of a (a). One half a sphere is called a (b). Line segment AC shows the (c) on which the sphere rotates.

2. The distance around the sphere is its (a). Line segment BD represents its (b).

3. In Figure 2, line segment MN is the angle bisector because it ____ the right angle.

4. Figure 3 is a model of a (a). Each base of this figure has a (b) shape. The measurement 1″ is the (c) height of the cylinder.

PROGRESS CHECK

WORD CHALLENGE

In a dictionary, find the meaning of each mathematical term below. Then sketch each figure to demonstrate your understanding of the term. Write the correct term under each figure that you draw.

pyramid	*trapezoid*
tetrahedron	*pentagon*
hexahedron	*octagon*

I am especially anxious
To raise the cash
And get permission
To see the collection
Of ancient machines.

SOUNDS and PATTERNS

1. Read the sentence below. Write the words in which you hear /sh/. Underline the letters that spell /sh/.

Please mention the cash in the machines.

2. In which other words is /sh/ spelled as in

a. cash? **b.** mention?

3. Copy the words you see below in italics. Underline the letters that spell /sh/.

We *shake* hands to express friendship. In *ancient* times, extending one's right hand meant that there was no weapon in it. This friendly *action* made no one *anxious* about foul play.

When /sh/ begins or ends a word, the /sh/ is usually spelled with the letters *sh*. Sometimes it is spelled with *ch, ti, si, ssi, ci,* or *xi.*

4. Study the spelling patterns below. Write each word as a column heading. Under each, write the list words with the same spelling pattern.

/shəl/ social	/shən/ action	/shən/ expression

shake
cash
action
section
mention
attention
condition
collection
expression
permission
machines
anxious
ancient
social
special
especially

shake
cash
action
section
mention
attention
condition
collection
expression
permission
machines
anxious
ancient
social
special
especially

STRUCTURE and MEANING

1. Copy each base word below. Beside each word, write the list word that is a derived form.

a. act **b.** collect **c.** express **d.** permit **e.** attend

2. Notice the use of the word *friend* in the first sentence below. Then note the difference in the use of the *ly* form of *friend* in the second sentence.

We knew the officer was our friend.
He had been sent by the prince on a friendly mission.

Write the following forms of base words to complete the sentences below.

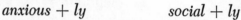

anxious + ly *social + ly*

a. We waited ____ for word of the men's rescue.
b. My brother is ____ at ease in large groups.

3. Write *special* and *especially* to complete the sentence.

I was ____ anxious to win the ____ prize.

4. ***DICTIONARY*** Write the words below in alphabetical order. Draw a line under the first letter in each word and extend the line to the letter that determines the place of that word in the alphabetical list of words. Use your Spelling Dictionary to check your accuracy.

shake *shock* *social* *shortage* *shield*

shock
shortage
shield
mission
pressure
fission
artificial
respiration
radiation

EXPANDING VOCABULARY Use words from both lists.

5. Write a list word that has nearly the same meaning as the italicized word or expression in the paragraph.

The scientist was given a government *assignment* to study the *giving off of rays* of a *certain* kind of atom. She wore a body *protector* made *exclusively* for the job. She was not given *consent* to tell anyone about her findings until her *store* of facts had been published by the government.

HANDWRITING Write the letters *i* and *t* carefully. Retrace the top stroke of both letters without making a loop. Dot the *i*. Carefully cross the *t*. Then write *attention* and *condition*.

i i t t
attention
condition

CHECK POINT They will choose some shoes to wear on their vacation trip to the ocean. Ⓢ

shock
shortage
shield
mission
pressure
fission
artificial
respiration
radiation

WORD KNOWLEDGE

1. Which list word comes from the Latin word *mittere*, meaning "to send"?

2. Which list words fit these definitions?

a. an insufficient supply
b. a protective covering
c. a sudden or violent jolt
d. the process of splitting into parts
e. the giving off of rays of energy, such as light or heat

3. Which list words complete these sentences?

a. The ____ from the sun's rays can be harmful to human tissue.
b. The activity of yeast cells is an example of ____.

4. Use list words to complete this paragraph:

The first-aid worker is trying to revive this boy. He is using (a) (b) by applying (c) to the boy's rib cage.

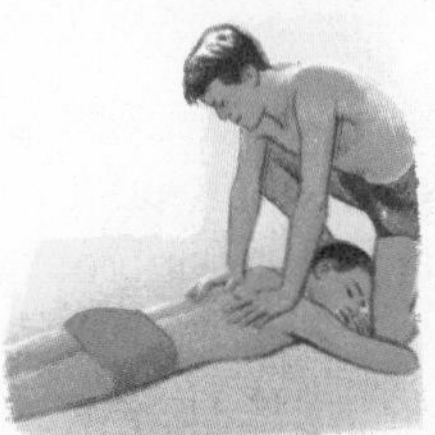

PROGRESS CHECK

WORD CHALLENGE

The words *fission* and *fusion* have different origins and therefore different meanings.

a. Write the meaning of each word.
b. Look up the word *fission* in an encyclopedia or science book. Tell how fission is used in the study of biology and physics.

REVIEW and EXTENSION 24

truck
quilt
yolks
hike

staff
herself
tough
paragraph

exchange
garbage
guest
gadget

stress
seventh
lace
scene

dash
information
aggression
racial

SOUNDS and PATTERNS

1. Say the words in the box. Listen for /k/.
   a. Which letter or letters spell /k/?
   b. Write two list words that end with /k/.

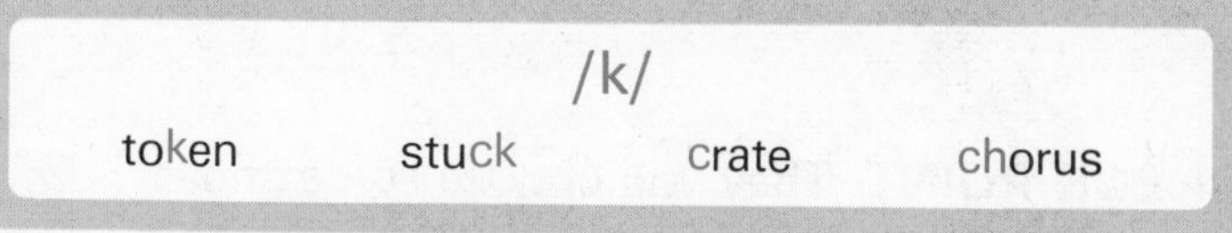

2. Write list words with the following sounds.
   a. /ks/ as in *tax* and *marks* b. /kw/ as in *quit*

3. Say each word below. Write the list words in which you hear /f/. Underline the letters that spell /f/.

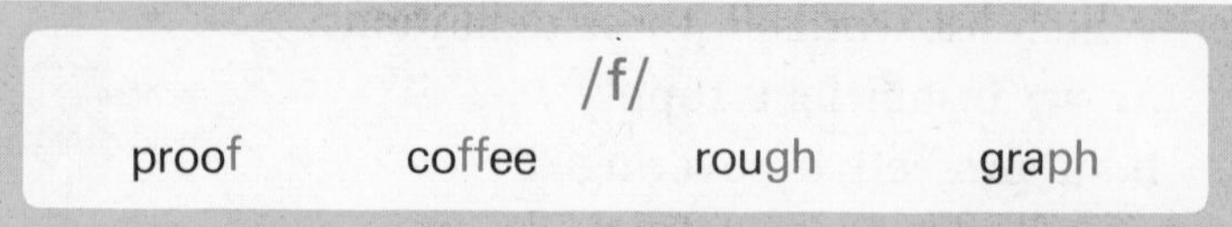

4. Say the words below. Listen for /j/ and /g/.

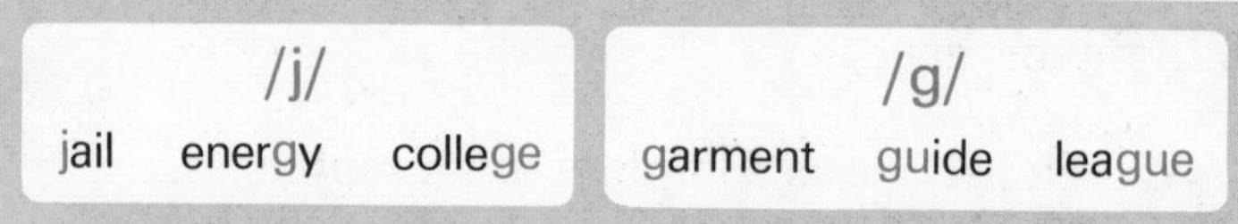

   a. Write the list words in which you hear /j/.
   b. In which list words do you hear /g/? Check (✓) the words in which you hear both /j/ and /g/.

5. Notice the letters below that spell /s/ and /sh/.

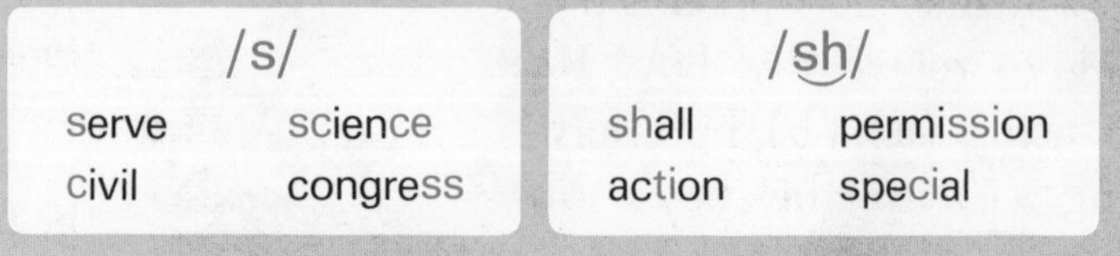

/s/
serve
science
civil
congress
/sh/
shall
permission
action
special

   a. Write any eight list words in which you hear /s/.
   b. In which list words do you hear /sh/?

DICTIONARY

1. Suppose that the guide words on page 120 of a dictionary were *salt* and *several* and that the guide words on page 121 were *sew* and *spell*. For each word below, write *120* or *121* to show on which page the word would appear.

a. special	**b.** satisfactory
c. soldier	**d.** semester
e. scenery	**f.** sincerely
g. shake	**h.** section

2. Say each entry word at the right.

a. Which word has five syllables?

b. Which word has four syllables?

3. Write each word below. After each, tell how many different meanings are given in the entry.

a. lack **b.** minister **c.** cycle

4. Write each italicized word below. After each, write the numeral of the definition that matches the meaning in the sentence.

a. The *scene* of the opera was medieval.

b. Our seats were in the *orchestra*.

5. Read the entries for *rock*[1] and *rock*[2]. Then read the sentence below. Which of the entries includes the meaning of *rock* that is used in the following sentence?

Please help me rock this stone loose.

CHECK POINT

If you misspelled words in Units 19–23, decide why you made errors. Study those words again. Then study the new words.

an nu al ly (an′ yů ə lē), *adv.* Once a year. [From Latin *annus* year.] —*Syn.* **yearly.**

cy cle (sī′ kəl), *n.* A series of events that repeat themselves, each time in the same order. The cocoon is one phase in the life *cycle* of the butterfly.

lack (lak), *n.* A want; a need that is not met. —*v.* To be without; to be wanting.

min is ter (min′ ə stər), *n.* 1. A cleric serving a church. 2. A person who is given charge of a department of the government. —*v.* To attend to comfort or wants; to be of service. She *ministered* to the sick man's wants.

or ches tra (ôr′ kə strə), *n.* 1. A group of musicians who perform as a unit. 2. The main floor of a theater.

rock[1] (rok), *n.* 1. A stone. 2. Something firm, like a rock. [From Old French *roque* rock.]

rock[2] (rok), *v.* Move back and forth; sway from side to side; tip up and down. [From Old English *roccian* to rock, to shake.]

scene (sēn), *n.* 1. A view; what can be seen. 2. The place, time, etc., of a story or drama. 3. A division of a drama.

vo cab u lar y (vō kab′ yə ler′ ē), *n.* The stock of words used in a language.

trucks
dashes
successes
exchanges
gadgets
paragraphs
staffs
yourselves
disarrange
disadvantage
misguide
rocky
wealthy
wealthiest
keener
toughest

WORD STRUCTURE

1. Study each base word and its plural form below.

boss	bosses	belief	beliefs
coach	coaches	knife	knives

a. Write the plural form of each word below. Underline the letter or letters that make each word plural.

exchange *truck* *success* *dash* *gadget*

b. Write the plural form of each word below.

paragraph *yourself* *staff*

2. Prefixes can form antonyms of base words.

continue	discontinue	handle	mishandle

Write list words that are antonyms of these words:

a. advantage **b.** arrange **c.** guide

3. Some words have derived forms ending with *y*. Notice the word in the box. Which list word is the derived form of the word in parentheses in each of the following phrases:

health + y ⟶ healthy

a. the (rock) trail **b.** a (wealth) person

4. Some words have more than one suffix.

kind	kinder	kindest	
health	healthy	healthier	healthiest

Which list word completes each group of words?

a. keen, ____, keenest **b.** tough, tougher, ____

c. wealth, wealthy, wealthier, ____

PROGRESS CHECK

Be sure you can spell all the words in the first lists from Units 19–24.

cycle
section
scenery
catalogue
press
knowledge
industry
thus
account
machines
scene
ache
semester
yourself
vegetables
enough
else
soldier

ON YOUR OWN

1. Complete the puzzle with list words.

Across

1. a part of
2. school term
6. other
7. period of time
8. so

Down

1. landscape
3. a view
4. sufficient
5. to iron

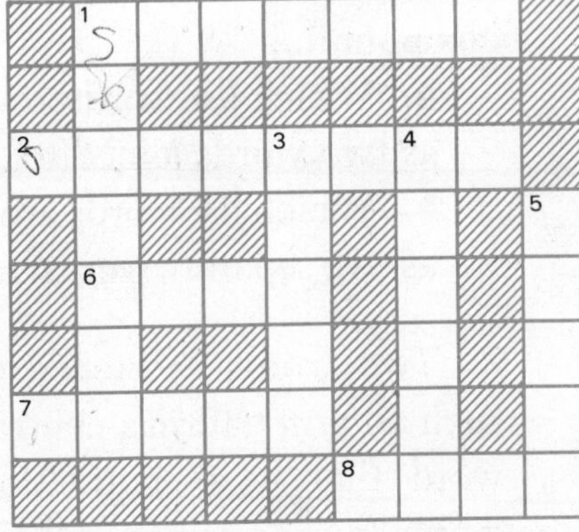

2. Write list words that contain the words below. Here is an example: *old—soldier*

a. count **b.** he **c.** log **d.** tables
e. chin **f.** our **g.** dust **h.** ledge

infirmary
shield
cylinder
terrific
jewels
specific

3. Write the word from the lettered sentence that completes the sentence that follows it.

a. She inserted the rolled map into the cylinder.
The mechanic installed a piston in the ____.

b. The knight's shield was shiny.
I must ____ my face from the sun.

4. Write list words that complete the poem.

Just think what we found! No, it wasn't a rock
But an old Spanish ship, with a treasure ____.
'Twas a box full of ____, to be more ____.

25

On a high school chalkboard
Bookkeepers keep track of time.
They've strawberry chalk in the A.M.
In the P.M., the flavor is lime!

within
however
therefore
bookkeeper
outline
high school
chalkboard
headache
per cent
etc.
P.S.
P.M.
they've
you're
one's
man's

SOUNDS and PATTERNS

1. A word formed from two or more words is a **compound.**

- **a.** Which list words are compounds written as two words joined together?
- **b.** Which list words are compounds written as two separate words?

2. Two words shortened into a single word, such as *hasn't,* form a **contraction.** Write the list word that is a contraction of the italicized words in each sentence.

- **a.** I hope *you are* planning to help us.
- **b.** We heard that *they have* moved.
- **c.** Which *one is* your brother?
- **d.** That *man is* my neighbor.

3. In Exercise **2,** which letters are left out of the shortened forms of *you are, they have,* and *one is?*

The apostrophe in a contraction shows where one or more letters have been left out.

4. A shortened form of a word, such as *Mr.,* is an **abbreviation.** Some abbreviations are written without periods. Write the abbreviations that appear in the word list.

STRUCTURE and MEANING

1. Write two contractions that could have been used in this sentence:

   You are the one they have chosen to lead the parade at tomorrow's football game.

2. A form of a word that shows someone owns something is a **possessive** word. An apostrophe sometimes shows ownership. Write a list word to replace each italicized phrase below.

   a. the hat *of the man* **b.** paper *that belongs to one*

3. Write the list word that has double consonant letters. Complete this sentence with the possessive form of the word.

   The ____ accounts are always accurate.

4. Which two list words correctly complete these sentences?

   I planned to help; ____, my headache grew worse, and ____ I was forced to stay home.

5. Write the abbreviations for these Latin expressions:

   a. *et cetera,* meaning "and other things"
   b. *post scriptum,* meaning "after the writing"
   c. *post meridiem,* meaning "after noon"

6. ***DICTIONARY*** Abbreviations are often listed alphabetically with entry words. The word *region,* for example, is entered before *R.F.D.* because *re* comes before the letters *rf.*

   Write *P.S., P.M., program,* and *per cent* in alphabetical order. Think of each word or abbreviation letter by letter.

within
however
therefore
bookkeeper
outline
high school
chalkboard
headache
per cent
etc.
P.S.
P.M.
they've
you're
one's
man's

COMPOUNDS

Use words from both lists.

7. By interchanging the parts of *without* and *lineup,* you can form the compound *outline*. Form as many compounds as you can from each pair of words below.

   a. headboard, backache **b.** headline, outboard
   c. turntable, sometime **d.** silverware, household

flatcar
countryside
sidetrack
switchyard
yardmaster
overdue
timetable
warehouse
headquarters

they've

you're

one's

HANDWRITING When writing contractions, always insert the apostrophe after completing the word. The apostrophe looks somewhat like a comma above the line. Write *they've*, *you're*, and *one's*.

flatcar
countryside
sidetrack
switchyard
yardmaster
overdue
timetable
warehouse
headquarters

CHECK POINT Won't somebody offer to go to the post office again next Wednesday? J

WORD KNOWLEDGE

1. Complete the paragraph with list words.

This freight train, passing through the quiet (a), is carrying one open car without sides, called a (b). The train is on a strict (c). To prevent it from being (d), other trains can be switched to a (e) to let it pass by.

2. Which list words complete these sentences?

a. A ____ directs railroad cars in a ____.

b. Goods stored in the ____ are recorded at the company ____.

WORD CHALLENGE

Inventions often result in the creation of new words and new meanings for old words. Many of these words are compounds.

Make a list of compounds related to space travel. The following words are used in compounds. Perhaps you can think of others.

air *space* *lift*

PROGRESS CHECK

26 Past-Tense Forms

They were interested; they dated.
They married; we were elated.
We wondered if the decorated cake
All trimmed with frosting
Was real or fake.

SOUNDS and PATTERNS

1. Study the spelling patterns described below.

a. Present tense ends with two consonant letters: *interest.* Past tense: *interested.*

b. Present tense ends with VC*e* pattern: *decorate.* Past tense: *decorated.*

c. Present tense ends with consonant-*y* pattern: *marry.* Past tense: *married.*

Head three columns **a, b,** and **c.** Write all the list words that match the spelling patterns of the past-tense forms shown above.

2. All the base words below end in the VC pattern. Notice that the single-syllable word and the word with a final stressed syllable are each spelled with a double consonant before *ed.*

step + ed ⟶ stepped
permit + ed ⟶ permitted
suffer + ed ⟶ suffered

Say each base word below and think about whether the stress is on the final syllable. Write list words that are past-tense forms of the base words. Check the words in which you doubled the final consonant before adding *ed.*

a. trim **b.** wonder **c.** consider **d.** control **e.** regret

3. Which list words are past-tense forms of the words *choose, tear, awake, strike, forgive?*

attached
interested
arrived
decorated
married
buried
considered
wondered
trimmed
regretted
controlled
tore
chose
struck
awoke
forgave

attached
interested
arrived
decorated
married
buried
considered
wondered
trimmed
regretted
controlled
tore
chose
struck
awoke
forgave

STRUCTURE and MEANING

1. Look at the *ing* form of each base word in the box. Which letter is in the word *decorate* that is not in *decorating*?

bury	burying
decorate	decorating

If a base word ends in the VC*e* pattern, the *e* is not usually used in spelling the *ing* form.

2. Which form of the word in parentheses correctly completes each sentence below?

a. They are (arrive) now. **b.** John is (marry) Joan.

3. Study the words in the box. Notice each base word and each form that ends with *ing*. The word *drop* is a one-syllable word ending in the VC pattern. The word *begin* has a final stressed syllable in the VC pattern.

drop	dropping
begin	beginning

Write the *ing* forms of *trim, regret,* and *control.*

4. ***DICTIONARY*** Irregular forms are shown after an entry word. From your Spelling Dictionary, write the form of the word in parentheses that correctly completes each of the following sentences.

a. (choose) We ____ the paint yesterday. Our painter has ____ to mix the colors.

b. (tear) Who ____ the canvas? It was ____ last night.

c. (forgive) The principal ____ us because we had been in an accident. We were happy she had ____ us.

enforced
canceled
prohibited
submitted
referred
compelled
enlisted
occupied
qualified

PROOFREADING Use words from both lists.

5. Four words in the paragraph below are used incorrectly. Write the correct form of each word.

When we arrive last night, the club room was occupy. We cancel the meeting after waiting ten minutes for another room. We then choose another date for the meeting.

HANDWRITING The final letter in a word should end with an upward stroke. Practice writing the letters *d, e, g, y,* and *r.* These are often the final letters in words. Then practice writing the words *arrived* and *chose.*

d e g y r

arrived

chose

CHECK POINT I have read that a library is planned, though it won't be built this year. (T)

enforced
canceled
prohibited
submitted
referred
compelled
enlisted
occupied
qualified

WORD KNOWLEDGE

1. Which word completes each sentence?

a. (enforced, compelled) The trooper ___ the speed limit. We were ___ to obey it.

b. (canceled, prohibited) Heavy rains ___ completion of the expressway. Therefore, the dedication ceremonies were ___.

2. Write a list word that correctly replaces the words in italics.

a. The mayor *turned back* to the most recent report. Then she *got the support of* a qualified engineer to outline the project.

b. Jay *offered* his application, hoping that he was *eligible* for the job.

3. Which list word completes this sentence? Her time is ___ with sports each fall.

PROGRESS CHECK

WORD CHALLENGE

Build as many English words as you can from the Latin root words *ferre,* meaning "to carry," and *pellere,* meaning "to drive." Use the following prefixes in building your words.

com (with)	*pre* (before)
de (from)	*pro* (forward)
ex (out of)	*re* (back)

27

Happiness! Lots of excitement
Coming from every direction.
An army of happy children
Have passed the examination.

election
protection
direction
education
transportation
examination
carriage
marriage
equipment
government
excitement
delivery
army
goodness
business
happiness

SOUNDS and PATTERNS

1. Write list words derived from these words:

a. elect **b.** direct **c.** educate
d. protect **e.** examine **f.** transport

2. In the following sentence, what part of speech is *elect? election?*

We elect our mayor in the November election.

3. Which list words end with the suffix *ment* or with the suffix *y*?

> The suffixes *ion, tion, ation, ment,* and *y* often form nouns when added to base words.

4. Look at the sentences below. Compare the spelling of *busy* with *business.*

They are busy people. Their business is successful.

a. Which letter in *busy* is not in *business?*
b. Write the word *business.*

5. Write list words derived from the following base words. Underline the letters in each derived form that are not in the base word.

a. happy **b.** marry **c.** carry

6. Write the list word derived from *good.*

STRUCTURE and MEANING

1. Study the following review of the spelling changes that result when a suffix is added to a base word.

> If a base word ends with a consonant + *y*, the past-tense form or the plural form is spelled by changing the *y* to *i* before adding the suffix.
>
> If a base word ends with a VC pattern in a stressed syllable, the final consonant is doubled before adding a suffix beginning with a vowel letter.

Write words that complete the sentences below. Use the correct forms of the words in parentheses.

- **a.** (equip) The city is ___ the playground with swings.
- **b.** (carry) Juan has ___ the groceries almost a mile.
- **c.** (army) Both ___ have agreed to observe the truce.
- **d.** (delivery) The store made two ___ today.

2. Write the *ly* form of each word in parentheses to complete each sentence.

- **a.** (happy) The children played ___ all day long.
- **b.** (busy) They worked ___ making the tree house.

3. ***DICTIONARY*** Write the following list words. Then draw a curved line under the letters that spell each syllable. Check your work by using the Spelling Dictionary.

a. government **b.** business **c.** examination **d.** election

election
protection
direction
education
transportation
examination
carriage
marriage
equipment
government
excitement
delivery
army
goodness
business
happiness

WRITING TITLES

Use words from both lists.

4. The title of a report gives a clue to the subject discussed in the report. Which list word could be used as a title for a report suggested by each group of words below?

- **a.** canoes, covered wagons, subways, airplanes
- **b.** pony express, radio, magazines, television, newspapers
- **c.** democracy, socialism, dictatorship, monarchy

preparation
communication
civilization
showmanship
sportsmanship
scholarship
necessity
modesty
privacy

T T G G
Transportation
Government

HANDWRITING Do you write capital *T* and *G* legibly? Practice writing the capital letters *T* and *G*. Notice that both letters end with the same stroke. Then practice writing *Transportation* and *Government*.

preparation
communication
civilization
showmanship
sportsmanship
scholarship
necessity
modesty
privacy

CHECK POINT Selections from many truly great plays made up their entertainment. Ⓤ

WORD KNOWLEDGE

1. Which list word best describes each quality below? The pictures are suggestive of each of these qualities.

a. a knowledge acquired by much study
b. a sense of fair play
c. ability to entertain

2. Write a list word that is similar in meaning to each word or phrase in the list below.

a. advanced culture **b.** readiness
c. exchange of information **d.** seclusion
e. requirement **f.** humbleness

PROGRESS CHECK

WORD CHALLENGE

Find the Latin origins of the root words for *communication* and *civilization* in your Spelling Dictionary. Head a column with each Latin root word. List as many other words as you can that come from the same source.

A dog can be a valuable companion if you're lonesome. You'll probably be successful if you make him comfortable and feed him daily.

comfortable
valuable
expensive
attractive
willing
cheerful
successful
lonesome
hungry
angry
greatly
finally
probably
exactly
easily
daily

SOUNDS and PATTERNS

1. Study the words in the box. Which letter was dropped from each base word before the suffix was added?

value	valuable
expense	expensive

When a suffix beginning with a vowel letter is added to a word ending with *e*, the *e* is usually dropped before adding the suffix.

2. Write list words derived from these words:
a. attract **b.** expense **c.** value **d.** comfort

3. Which list words end with these suffixes?
a. *ing* **b.** *some* **c.** *ful*

4. Study the words in the box. Write all list words that fit these descriptions:

final	finally
easy	easily
probable	probably

a. Usually, the spelling of a base word is not changed when the suffix *ly* is added.
b. If a base word ends with *y*, the *y* is changed to *i* before *ly* is added.
c. If a base word ends with *le*, the *le* is usually dropped before *ly* is added.

5. Which list word is derived from *anger*? from *hunger*? How many syllables are in each word?

comfortable
valuable
expensive
attractive
willing
cheerful
successful
lonesome
hungry
angry
greatly
finally
probably
exactly
easily
daily

STRUCTURE and MEANING

1. Write the following words. Pronounce each word carefully. Write the number of syllables you hear in each word.

a. comfortable **b.** finally **c.** easily
d. valuable **e.** probably **f.** exactly

2. Write a list word that means the same as the italicized word or phrase in each sentence below.

a. He arranges *very pleasing* window displays *every day.*
b. The man was *filled with anger* at the *costly* rentals.

3. Which list word is an antonym of each of these words?

a. unsuccessful **b.** inexpensive **c.** unwilling

4. Write the form of the word in parentheses that correctly completes each sentence.

a. (value) The painting was very ____.
b. (comfort) We are most ____ in slacks.

5. ***DICTIONARY*** Many suffixes have entries in your Spelling Dictionary. Notice the suffix entry in the box. It shows the meanings of the suffix and the part of speech the suffix helps to form.

> -y, *adj. suffix.* 1. Having. 2. Being like.

Find the suffix *ful* in your Spelling Dictionary. Notice that, unlike the word *full,* the suffix has only one *l.*

a. Write the meaning of the suffix *ful.*
b. Find the suffix *ive.* Write its meaning.
c. What part of speech may end with the suffix *ive?*

triangular
rectangular
yearly
annually
semiannually
biannually
associative
commutative
distributive

DESCRIPTIVE WORDS

Use words from both lists.

6. Write the word that best describes each of the following.

a. one who is charming but not necessarily beautiful
b. a person who has no objections to performing a duty
c. something that has three sides
d. a person who longs for a friend

HANDWRITING The letter *y* should be carefully written. Notice that *y* begins with a round hump, like *n*. The loop should be kept on a slant and should cross on the base line. Practice writing *y*. Then write *angry* and *easily*.

y y y
angry
easily

CHECK POINT He says a handy tear strip does seem useful enough for opening cans.

triangular
rectangular
yearly
annually
semiannually
biannually
associative
commutative
distributive

WORD KNOWLEDGE

1. Write the list word that comes from the Latin word *annus,* meaning "year." Then write the list word that is a synonym of this word.

2. Write the list word that means "every six months" or "every half year." Underline the prefix that means "half."

3. Write the list word that means "twice a year."

4. The number sentences in the box at the right show three mathematical principles. Three list words name these principles.

a. $4 + 6 = 6 + 4$
b. $(3 + 2) + 5 = 3 + (2 + 5)$
c. $3 \times 6 = (3 \times 2) + (3 \times 4)$

Write the letters **a, b,** and **c.** Next to each letter, write the name of the mathematical principle illustrated in the box.

5. Write the letters **a** and **b.** Next to each letter, write the word that describes the matching geometric figure.

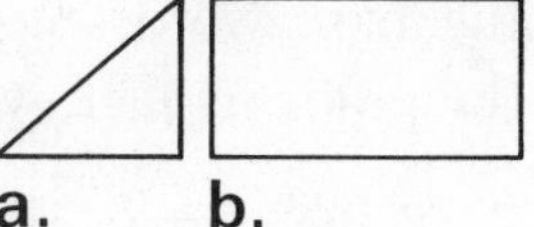

PROGRESS CHECK

WORD CHALLENGE

1. Two English words that name periods of time come from the Latin words *centum,* meaning "hundred," and *mille,* meaning "thousand." Using this information, write the meanings of:
a. century **b.** millennium

2. What is a *bicentennial?* Try to write your own meaning. Then check it with a dictionary.

29

Unattended, my cat made a mistake. He was just too independent. Now he's really ashamed. He'll never descend into the fish bowl again.

impossible
improper
independent
incorrect
unattended
undecided
mistake
misspell
ashamed
aside
disagree
disrespect
describe
descend
require
request

SOUNDS and PATTERNS

1. Write the list words that begin with /ə/. Underline the letter that spells this sound in each word.

2. Write the list word for each respelling below.

a. (in′ kə rekt′) **b.** (im prop′ ər) **c.** (un′ ə ten′ did)

3. What do the prefixes *in, im,* and *un* mean?

4. Write the other list words that begin with the prefixes *in, im,* and *un.*

5. The prefix *mis* means "wrong." Notice the spelling of the word in the box that begins with *mis.* Copy the word formed from *mis* + *spell.*

mis + *spell* → misspell

Write another list word that begins with the prefix *mis.*

6. Write the list words that are formed from the base words *respect* and *agree.* Underline the prefix in each word.

7. Which list words begin with the prefix *de*?

8. The prefix *re* means "back" or "again." Write the list words that begin with *re.*

STRUCTURE and MEANING

1. Write the list word that means the same as the italicized phrase in each sentence. Underline the prefix in each word.

a. Skiing is *not possible* now. **b.** It is *not correct.*
c. The patient was *not attended.* **d.** Slang is *not proper.*

2. Write the list word that can be an antonym for:

a. agree **b.** correct **c.** proper **d.** respect

An antonym can be formed from a prefix + a base word.

3. Add a prefix to each word below.

a. dependent **b.** attended **c.** possible

4. Two list words come from the Latin *re,* meaning "back," and *quaerere,* meaning "to ask." Write these two words.

5. Which list word comes from the Latin prefix *de,* meaning "down," and the root word *scandere,* meaning "to climb"?

6. ***DICTIONARY*** The box shows the pronunciation for the entry word *incorrect.* In the respelling, the heavier mark, or the **primary stress mark,** shows the syllable with more stress. The lighter mark, or **secondary stress mark,** shows the syllable with less stress.

in cor rect (in′ kə rekt′)

Write the following words. Draw a curved line under the letters that spell each syllable having primary stress.

a. disagree **b.** disrespect

impossible
improper
independent
incorrect
unattended
undecided
mistake
misspell
ashamed
aside
disagree
disrespect
describe
descend
require
request

THE EXACT WORD

Use words from both lists.

7. Write the word that best describes each person or action.

a. pushing ahead of someone else in a cafeteria line
b. making a decision without asking anyone's opinion
c. a person who often moves from place to place
d. a person whose mind is not made up

decrease
increase
transact
transient
transatlantic
transcontinental
interstate
international
interplanetary

aside
independent
undecided

HANDWRITING Be sure to close *a* and *d*. Practice writing the words *aside, independent,* and *undecided*. Check each word to make sure each letter is clearly written.

decrease
increase
transact
transient
transatlantic
transcontinental
interstate
international
interplanetary

CHECK POINT I always dislike writing letters, but I am unable to avoid it in my business. E

WORD KNOWLEDGE

1. The prefix *trans* means "across." The prefix *inter* means "between." Describe each flight below with two list words.

a. New York to Paris **b.** Boston to Seattle

2. Which list word describes a rocket flight between two planets?

3. Write the list word that begins with the prefix *trans* and correctly completes each phrase.

a. to ___ business **b.** ___ laborer

4. Which word fits each definition below?

a. to grow larger **b.** to grow or become less

PROGRESS CHECK

WORD CHALLENGE

Write as many words as you can, using the Latin prefixes listed below with the following Latin root words: *mittere*, meaning "to send," *quaerere*, meaning "to ask," and *scribere*, meaning "to write."

sub	*trans*	*com*
re	*de*	*in*

30 REVIEW and EXTENSION

whatever
newspaper
otherwise
that's

inquired
attended
equipped
delivered

kindness
directory
assignment
description

lonely
dependable
respectful
descriptive

abroad
uncomfortable
inexpensive
misunderstand

SOUNDS and PATTERNS

1. The paragraph below contains three list words that are compounds. Write the three compounds.

Our newspaper editor demands that whatever is printed must contain correct facts. It cannot be otherwise.

2. Which contraction can replace the italicized words in the sentence below?

We know *that is* correct. We checked the facts.

3. Study each base word and its past-tense form below.

consider	arrive	control
considered	arrived	controlled

Write each word below and then its *ed* form.

a. deliver **b.** inquire **c.** attend **d.** equip

4. A form of each word below appears in the word list. Write the list word. Underline the suffix or the prefix in each word.

a. kind **b.** lone **c.** assign
d. understand **e.** respect **f.** depend

5. Write the list word that is a derived form of each word in parentheses.

a. (expense) sweater **b.** (comfort) chair

6. Two list words are derived from *describe.* Write the word that correctly completes each phrase.

a. a vivid ____ **b.** a ____ report of the game

7. Write the list word that fits each definition below. After each word, write the number of syllables it has.

a. that which directs **b.** outside one's country

–able, *adj. suffix.* 1. Worthy of. 2. Able to.

book keep er (bu̇k′ kē′ pər), *n.* A person whose job is keeping records of business matters.

di rec tion (də rek′ shən), *n.* 1. A rule for doing or making something. 2. The line in which something is moving or facing. 3. That which a compass shows.

man's¹, *contraction.* Man is.

man's², *possessive.* Of a man, or person.

mis un der stand (mis′ un dər stand′), *v.* To understand wrongly; to fail to understand.

re gret (ri gret′), *v.*, **regretted, regretting.** To feel sorry about.

strike (strīk), *v.*, **struck, striking.** 1. To hit. 2. To remove or cancel. *Strike* a name from the list. 3. To quit work in order to force some change in the conditions of employment. —*n.* The act of striking.

DICTIONARY

1. Suppose you were to insert the abbreviation *m.p.h.* into the column at the left. Think about the alphabetical order of dictionary entries. After which word would you insert *m.p.h.*?

2. Write *bookkeeper* and *misunderstand*. Draw a curved line under the letters that spell each syllable having primary stress.

3. Write the numeral for the definition of the word *direction* that matches the meaning of the italicized word in the sentence below.

Blanche made a miniature castle by following the *directions* given in the model kit.

4. Find the entry for the suffix *able*.

a. How many meanings are shown?

b. What part of speech may end with *able*?

5. Write the form of *strike* that correctly completes each sentence.

a. They are ____ the error from the record.

b. The runaway sled ____ a tree.

6. Write *1* or *2* to tell which entry for *man's* fits the meaning of the word in each sentence.

a. I heard a man's voice.

b. That man's very tall.

7. Read the entry for *regret* at the left. Write the other forms of *regret* that are shown.

CHECK POINT

If you misspelled words in Units 25–29, decide why you made errors. Study those words again. Then study the new words.

WORD STRUCTURE

1. Study the derived forms of *protect*. Notice that a word may have more than one suffix.

protect + ion ⟶	protection
protect + ive + ly ⟶	protectively

Write the list words that are derived forms of the words below. Underline the suffix or suffixes in each word.

a. consider **b.** decorate **c.** attract **d.** elect

2. Study the base word *happy* and its derived form. Then write the list word that is a form of each of these words:

a. lonely **b.** cheerful **c.** lonesome

happy
happiness

3. Study the following verb forms.

request	requested	has requested
shake	shook	has shaken

Write the list word that is a form of the word in parentheses in each phrase below.

a. (misspell) the word **b.** (descend) the ladder
c. has (tear) the paper **d.** has (choose) a color
e. was (forgive) for his mistake

4. Write the two list words that are contractions. After each contraction, write the words it stands for.

5. Answer the questions below with list words.

a. The symbol % stands for what compound?
b. What is the abbreviation of *and so forth?*

elective
decorative
decoration
consideration
decoratively
attractively
cheerfulness
lonesomeness
loneliness
torn
chosen
forgiven
descended
misspelled
you're
they've
etc.
per cent

undecided
cheerful
finally
impossible
equipment
excitement
disagree
arrived
mistake
struck
election
outline
chose
within
misspell
exactly

PROGRESS CHECK

Be sure you can spell all the words in the first lists from Units 25–30.

ON YOUR OWN

1. Write the list word that can replace the italicized word or phrase in each sentence.

- **a.** I *decided* to return the package when it *came* too late.
- **b.** We needed special *tools* for the shop.
- **c.** Try not to repeat that *error.*
- **d.** *At last* we reached a proper decision.
- **e.** The house was painted blue *on the inside.*

2. Form list words from the prefixes and base words.
Prefixes: *mis im dis un*
Base Words: *agree decided spell possible*

3. Form list words from the base words and suffixes.
Base Words: *cheer excite exact elect*
Suffixes: *ly ful ion ment*

4. Write the word from the lettered sentence that completes the sentence that follows it.

- **a.** The house was struck by lightning.
  The teachers ____ for smaller classes.
- **b.** The class was told to outline the story.
  Angela sketched an ____ of the building.

associative
timetable
submitted
distributive
occupied
commutative
scholarship

5. Which list word answers each riddle?

- **a.** What has a pie but no crust?
- **b.** What has a ship but no rudders?
- **c.** What has a table but no chairs?
- **d.** What has a mitt but no ball?

6. Write the words that are mathematical terms.

A horse had a pain in his sole.
Stepping on tacks made a hole!
A sore foot for a week
Left him terribly weak,
But his spirit and soul were whole!

SOUNDS and PATTERNS

week
horse
hole
cents

1. Say each word in the box.
   a. Write a list word that sounds the same as each word in the box.
   b. Do the spellings of the words you wrote match the spellings of the words in the box?
   c. Are the words you wrote synonyms, antonyms, or homophones of the words in the box?

Words that sound alike but have different meanings and spellings are homophones.

2. Which list word is a homophone of each word below? Put a check mark (✓) after the word that is a contraction.
   a. tacks b. soar c. weave d. sole

3. Write a pair of words for each respelling. Underline the letters that spell the same sound or sounds in different ways.
   a. (koun′ səl) b. (prin′ sə pəl)
   c. (sta′ shə ner′ ē)

4. Write the list words that rhyme with the words below. Then underline the letters that spell /ā/.
   a. cane b. late

pain
sore
sense
soul
tax
we've
weak
whole
hoarse
straight
council
counsel
principle
principal
stationary
stationery

pain
sore
sense
soul
tax
we've
weak
whole
hoarse
straight
council
counsel
principle
principal
stationary
stationery

STRUCTURE and MEANING

1. The first sentence in each pair of sentences below contains the homophone of a word that can be used to complete the second sentence. Write each pair of homophones.

a. There is a holiday this week. That coffee looks ____.

b. Did you see that jet soar almost straight up? Too much shouting will give you a ____ throat.

c. This whole box of candy still costs just fifty cents. It doesn't make ____ to pay double the price.

2. Think about the meanings of the homophones in parentheses. Then write the homophone that correctly completes each sentence.

a. (principle, principal) The school ____ spoke to us.

b. (stationary, stationery) This is not expensive ____.

3. Use the *ful* form of a list word to complete the sentence.

The sprain was very ____.

4. Write the *ly* form of the list word that means the same as the word in italics.

Jean's interest is *mainly* in sports.

5. Write the list word that is a contraction. Then write the two words from which it was formed.

pier
peer
berth
hangar
ferry
brake
knight
altar
alter

6. ***DICTIONARY*** Look up the definitions of the words *counsel* and *council* in your Spelling Dictionary. Then write the word that correctly completes each sentence. After each word, write its part of speech.

a. The ____ must rewrite the rules for hall monitors.

b. The principal will ____ us in making fair rules.

USING SUFFIXES — Use words from both lists.

7. Use a suffix with a list word to write a homophone for each word below.

a. weekly **b.** panes **c.** nightly **d.** holy

HANDWRITING The letter *w* ends with a slight upcurve. Remember this when you connect *w* to the next letter in a word. Practice writing *w*. Then practice writing the words *weak* and *whole*.

w w
weak
whole

W **CHECK POINT** My dear cousin is too busy to write and ask which color shoes I would like.

pier
peer
berth
hangar
ferry
brake
knight
altar
alter

WORD KNOWLEDGE

1. Write list words to complete the paragraph.

The space reserved for a ship at a pier is called a (a). The boat that is used to (b) people and vehicles across water docks at a slip. An airplane is housed in a (c).

2. Write homophones that correctly complete each pair of phrases below.

a. to ____ into darkness, a wooden ____

b. to ____ the skirt length, a church ____

3. Write the homophone for each incorrect word.

a. a car's foot break **b.** a night in armor

PROGRESS CHECK

WORD CHALLENGE

Write at least one homophone for each word below. Some words have two homophones. Learn the meaning of each word you write.

a. doe
b. core
c. right
d. rye
e. main
f. burrow
g. marshal
h. taught

32

Complete your contract soon,
Produce a perfect product,
Become an expert on perfumes
And make a scent from lily blooms.

subject
object
project
perfect
contract
conduct
discard
expert
export
produce
perfume
costume
graduate
separate
progress
associate

SOUNDS and PATTERNS

Words with the same spellings but different pronunciations and meanings are homographs.

1. Write each list word that is respelled below. After each word, write the letter of the phrase in which the homograph is used. If necessary, use your dictionary.

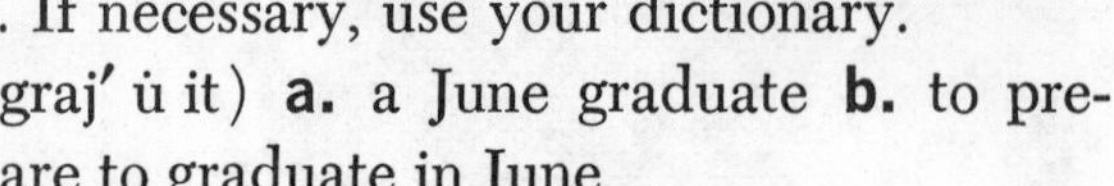

(graj′ ů it) **a.** a June graduate **b.** to prepare to graduate in June

(pėr′ fikt) **a.** to perfect a speech **b.** a perfect solution

(ə sō′ shē it) **a.** a business associate **b.** to associate with neighbors

(prə gres′) **a.** a century of progress **b.** to progress in mathematics

(proj′ ekt) **a.** a new project **b.** to project an idea into the future

(prə düs′) **a.** to produce **b.** farm produce

2. Write the two list words used in each sentence below. Then draw a curved line under the letters that spell each stressed syllable.

a. I'd like to discard this costume.
b. One French export is perfume.
c. Mother is an expert on that subject.
d. Do you object to Ray's conduct?
e. We drew up a separate contract.

STRUCTURE and MEANING

1. Write the list word that identifies each picture. Then underline each stressed syllable.

2. Write the *ion* form of each word in parentheses to complete each sentence correctly.

a. The high school (graduate) was held in the stadium.
b. We have no (object) to any of your suggestions.
c. My sister plays the piano with (perfect).
d. The school (product) was a success.
e. A (separate) from your family can prove to be lonely.

3. Write the *ing* form of each word in parentheses to complete each sentence correctly.

a. What is John (separate) on that table?
b. The factory is (produce) better motors this year.
c. Is Doris (progress) in her science class?
d. We have been (associate) with the older children.

4. ***DICTIONARY*** Find the entry for *separate* in your Spelling Dictionary. Notice the different parts of speech, pronunciations, and meanings.

Now write the word *separate* two times. After each word, write *adj.* or *v.* to tell its use in the sentence below.

He will separate the paper into separate stacks.

subject
object
project
perfect
contract
conduct
discard
expert
export
produce
perfume
costume
graduate
separate
progress
associate

PUZZLING SENTENCES Use words from both lists.

5. Each sentence below sounds puzzling until you find the word that completes it. Write the list word that completes each sentence.

a. If it weren't suitable, it wouldn't be ____.
b. Electricity wouldn't touch it, if it didn't ____.
c. If it isn't this choice, it's an ____.
d. No one would trip over it, if it didn't ____.

conflict
contrast
confine
protest
compress
rebel
appropriate
advocate
alternate

j j p p
project
perfect

HANDWRITING The letters *p* and *j* begin alike. The lower loops cross on the line. Close the final oval on *p* and curve the last stroke upward. Practice writing *j* and *p*. Then write *project* and *perfect*.

conflict
contrast
confine
protest
compress
rebel
appropriate
advocate
alternate

CHECK POINT I meant to raise a question about the loose records kept of the contest. Ⓧ

WORD KNOWLEDGE

1. Write the list word that belongs with each group of words below.

a. fitting, suitable, ____
b. enclose, restrict, ____
c. set off, show the difference, ____
d. squeeze, condense, ____

2. Write the list words that have these Latin origins:

a. *com* (together) + *premere* (to press)
b. *re* (again) + *bellum* (war)

3. Write the list words that best complete the following paragraph.

We do not agree with the proposed law. It is in (a) with our community plans. We hope our senator will (b) it and (c) a new bill in order to give the lawmakers an (d) choice. We do hope a more (e) bill will be considered.

4. Write a list word to complete each sentence.

a. A ____ is usually angry at someone.
b. A hot ____ sometimes helps a headache.

PROGRESS CHECK

WORD CHALLENGE

The terms below are often used in discussing politics and politicians. Write a sentence that explains the political meaning of each term. Use a dictionary or a history book if you need help.

a. filibuster **b.** maverick
c. lame duck **d.** lobbyist

33 Words Easily Confused

SOUNDS and PATTERNS

1. Write each pair of words below. Then check (✓) the word that answers each question.

a. (accept, except) Which word begins with /a/ spelled with the letter *a*?

b. (advise, advice) Which word ends with /z/? Underline the letter that spells /z/.

c. (adopt, adapt) Which word has a letter that spells /o/ in the final syllable?

2. Write the list word for each respelling.

a. (es kāp′) **b.** (ek sept′)
c. (ef′ ərt) **d.** (ek spekt′)

3. Say each word in the box. Look carefully at its spelling. Then write the list words that have spelling patterns similar to the words in the box.

when
wealth
infect
accident

4. Say *weather* and *whether*. Are these words homophones? Look at the dictionary respellings.

5. In which list words is a single consonant sound spelled with double consonant letters?

6. Read the sentence below, carefully saying each word that completes it. Write the words.

Our ____ was about ____ of forests.

7. Which list word rhymes with *four*?

accept
except
expect
escape
advice
advise
adopt
adapt
conversation
conservation
effect
effort
afford
weather
whether
pour

accept
except
expect
escape
advice
advise
adopt
adapt
conversation
conservation
effect
effort
afford
weather
whether
pour

STRUCTURE and MEANING

1. Write the form of *except* or *adopt* that correctly completes each sentence below.

a. Sometimes there should be an ___ to a rule.
b. The governor promises the ___ of new traffic laws.

2. Which list word is derived from each base word below?

a. converse **b.** conserve

3. Write the form of *expect* that completes this sentence: Our greatest ___ was to win the tournament.

4. Write the words that correctly complete each pair of sentences. Choose from these pairs of words:

advice, advise *adapt, adopt*
expect, except *weather, whether*

a. Didn't Dad ___ you about traffic laws for bike riders?
The coach gave us good ___, and we followed it.
b. Will the Collectors' Club ___ a new constitution?
Can anyone ___ the old rules to fit the new game?
c. Did you ___ to find a silver dollar?
Every marcher was out of step ___ Harry.
d. What kind of ___ is predicted for tomorrow?
Does anyone know ___ Aunt Clara will drive or fly?

serf
manor
canary
cannery
peasant
pheasant
feudal
futile
guild

5. ***DICTIONARY*** Find *conversation* in your Spelling Dictionary. Write the word. After it, write the number of syllables that are stressed in the word. Then draw a curved line under the letters of the syllable having primary stress.

DERIVED FORMS

Use words from both lists.

6. Write a form of each list word, using the suffix shown.

a. *accept + able* **b.** *advise + able*
c. *accept + ance* **d.** *escape + ism*
e. *feudal + ism* **f.** *futile + ity*

HANDWRITING Letters carelessly formed may appear as spelling errors. The letters *x*, *t*, and *c* are sometimes troublesome. Keep *c* open. Cross *t* and *x*. Write the words shown in the box. Make a rounded curve on *x*.

accept
expect
except

Y **CHECK POINT** My legs ache as if I had done forty separate laps around the whole field.

serf
manor
canary
cannery
peasant
pheasant
feudal
futile
guild

WORD KNOWLEDGE

1. Which list word fits each definition below?

a. colorful game bird
b. small singing bird, usually yellow

2. A factory where food is canned is a ___.

3. Read each sentence. Find each word that is used incorrectly. Then write the list word that correctly replaces it.

a. The cannery sang a sweet song.
b. A surf is almost a slave.
c. A peasant has colorful feathers.
d. Rover made a feudal effort to escape.

4. Complete each sentence with a list word.

In the (a) system of the Middle Ages, the lord owned the estate, or (b). The farmer who worked the land was a (c), or serf.

In the towns, a person learned a trade by joining a craft (d).

PROGRESS CHECK

WORD CHALLENGE

In the Middle Ages, craftsmen formed organizations called guilds. There were three classes of members in a craft guild: *master*, *journeyman*, and *apprentice*.

Write the medieval meanings of these three terms. Use an encyclopedia.

34 More Consonant Sounds

In my opinion, it would be hard to measure the pleasure Junior felt as he viewed the First Division of the Honor Guard marching toward the depot.

opinion
million
union
figure
junior
senior
garage
corsage
measure
pleasure
division
wrist
honor
honest
toward
depot

SOUNDS and PATTERNS

1. Say each word in the box. Which letter spells /y/ in *lawyer*? in *million*?

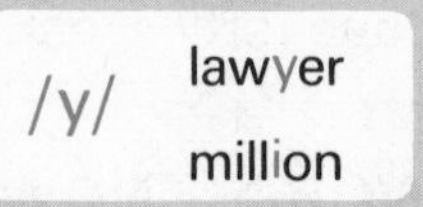

The /y/ may be spelled with *y* or *i*.

2. Write all the list words in which /y/ is spelled with *i*. Check (✓) the word in which /yü/ is spelled with *u*. Then write the word for this respelling: (fig′ yər).

3. Say each word in the box.

a. Write *garage, measure,* and *division.* Underline the letters that spell /zh/.

b. Which list word rhymes with *garage*? with *measure*?

/zh/
garage
measure
division

The /zh/ is often spelled with *ge* or *su*. The /zh/ is spelled with *si* in /zhən/.

4. Which list words begin with the sounds below? Underline the first written letter in each word.

a. /r/ **b.** /o/

5. Write the word for each of these respellings:

a. (tôrd) **b.** (dē′ pō)

STRUCTURE and MEANING

1. Write list words that complete the comparisons below.
   a. A bus stop is to a bus as a ____ is to a train.
   b. Crying is to sorrow as smiling is to ____.
   c. Increase is to decrease as multiplication is to ____.

2. Write the list word that has almost the same meaning as the phrase in italics in each sentence.
   a. The senator expressed a *personal view* of the law.
   b. Carlos was worthy of the medal of *high respect.*

3. Write one list word that completes each pair of sentences.
   a. The ____ 75 represents your score.
   Can you ____ out this puzzle?
   b. Bill will ____ the distance from here to the corner.
   Your ability to learn is beyond ____.

4. ***DICTIONARY*** A dictionary entry shows where a word can be divided at the end of a line of writing. Use a dictionary when you are not sure where to divide a word. A one-syllable word should not be divided. A single letter should not be on a line by itself.

   Look at the entries in the box.

o bey
cheer ful

   a. Should you divide the word *obey*?
   b. After which letter should you divide the word *cheerful*?
   c. Look at the list words. Which of the following words would you not syllabicate at the end of a line: *million, garage, honest, wrist*?

opinion
million
union
figure
junior
senior
garage
corsage
measure
pleasure
division
wrist
honor
honest
toward
depot

NONSENSE RHYMES

Use words from both lists.

5. Write the list word that completes each nonsense rhyme.
   a. How will we ____
   Such a treasure?
   b. Lose your ____
   And you're a goner.
   c. Let's spend Christmas
   On the ____.
   d. I see the ____
   Is a high riser.

billion
dominion
señor
fiord
geyser
glacier
isthmus
estuary
oasis

u n u n
union
junior

HANDWRITING Be sure that *u* and *n* can be distinguished from each other. Make a round hump on *n*. Start *u* like *i*. End each letter with an upstroke. Practice writing *u* and *n*. Then write *union* and *junior*.

billion
dominion
señor
fiord
geyser
glacier
isthmus
estuary
oasis

CHECK POINT Whether they win or lose three straight games, they will be welcome here. P

WORD KNOWLEDGE

1. Write the list word that belongs with each group of words below.

a. thousand, million, ____
b. mister, monsieur, ____
c. iceberg, icecap, ____

2. Read each description below of a geographic feature. Write the list word that names each geographic feature.

a. a strip of land with water on two sides and connecting two larger bodies of land
b. an inlet of the sea where the tide meets the river's current
c. a spot in the desert where there is water and vegetation
d. an inlet of the sea between high cliffs

3. Write a list word for each of the following descriptions.

a. a self-governing state of the British Commonwealth, such as Canada
b. a hot spring which at intervals throws a jet of hot water and steam into the air

PROGRESS CHECK

WORD CHALLENGE

Many of the world's great cities are near bodies of water. Write the name of each city listed below. After each, name the body of water the city is near. Use an atlas or an encyclopedia.

a. New York　　b. Cologne
c. Geneva　　d. Bangkok
e. Venice　　f. Cleveland

35 *Adjoining Vowel Sounds*

Which would you appreciate most?
Exercise in the gymnasium?
Violins playing in the auditorium?
A trip to the museum?
Or poetry reading in a quiet area?
KON TIKI

SOUNDS and PATTERNS

1. Say each word in the box.

hoe	poetry	cheap	realize

a. How many vowel sounds do the letters *oe* spell in *hoe*?

b. Write *poetry*. How many vowel sounds do the letters *oe* spell in *poetry*?

c. Which letters are written for /ē/ in *cheap*?

d. Write *realize*. How many vowel sounds do the letters *ea* spell in *realize*?

2. Write other list words in which *e* and *a* are written for two sounds, as in *realize*.

3. Write the list word for each respelling below.

a. (vī′ ə lin′) **b.** (mə tir′ ē əl)
c. (ā′ vē ā′ tər) **d.** (pir′ ē əd)
e. (myü zē′ əm) **f.** (ô′ də tôr′ ē əm)
g. (krü′ əl) **h.** (kwī′ ət)
i. (yü′ zhu̇ əl ē) **j.** (ə prē′ shē āt)

4. In which words is *y* written
a. for /ē/? **b.** for /i/?

poetry
violin
realize
idea
museum
usually
period
area
material
immediately
aviator
appreciate
auditorium
gymnasium
cruel
quiet

poetry
violin
realize
idea
museum
usually
period
area
material
immediately
aviator
appreciate
auditorium
gymnasium
cruel
quiet

STRUCTURE and MEANING

1. Write the list word that means almost the same as the italicized words in each sentence below.

a. This package will be delivered *without delay.*
b. The subscription runs for a one-year *span of time.*
c. The students *are grateful for* an extra holiday.
d. We *understand fully* why the rule has been made.

2. Write the list words that have the following Latin origins.

a. *audire,* meaning "to hear"
b. *appretiare,* meaning "to value"

3. Write the form of a list word that best completes each phrase below.

a. a letter of ____ **b.** disapprove of severe ____
c. ____ lyrics for the song **d.** has ____ one's ambition

4. Write a list word that completes each of the following comparisons.

a. Waitress is to waiter as aviatrix is to ____.
b. Theater is to drama as ____ is to basketball.
c. A key is to a piano as a bow is to a ____.

5. ***DICTIONARY*** Sometimes two respellings are shown after an entry word. Both pronunciations are correct.

In your Spelling Dictionary, find the words *aviator* and *auditorium.* Write each word. After each word, tell whether you use the first pronunciation shown or the second.

audio-visual
genuine
radiator
radium
uranium
vacuum
coaxial
amplifier
audience

PROOFREADING Use words from both lists.

6. The blanks show that one or more letters have been omitted from some words. Write these words correctly.

The mus_um is usua_y qu_t. But when the mater_ for the display cabinets came, the room was i_ediat_ly very noisy. Everyone showed gen_ne interest in the new equipment. Even the steam rad_t_r seemed to sing a little tune.

HANDWRITING The letters *a, e, i, o,* and *u* must be carefully formed so that they do not appear as spelling errors. Write each letter. Then join *a, e, i, o,* and *u.* Now write the words *idea* and *auditorium.*

a e i o u

idea

auditorium

CHECK POINT My throat is beginning to feel hoarse, so I must not stay among the crowd.

audio-visual
genuine
radiator
radium
uranium
vacuum
coaxial
amplifier
audience

WORD KNOWLEDGE

1. Write list words to complete the paragraphs.

The transmission of television to a nationwide (a) is complex. Part of the equipment used is a cable that transmits several signals at once. This cable is made up of smaller cables intertwined around a central core, or axis. Thus it gets its name, (b) cable.

The apparatus that increases, or amplifies, the strength of electric current is called an (c). The airless tubes in an amplifier are (d) tubes.

2. Write the list words to fit these meanings:

a. Two words naming chemical elements that give off radioactive rays. Check the one often used in medical treatments.

b. A device that gives off heat

3. Which list word comes from the Latin *audire,* meaning "to hear," + *videre,* meaning "to see"?

4. Which list word means "real"?

PROGRESS CHECK

WORD CHALLENGE

A manual describing a record player, or phonograph, uses the terms below. Write each term and then define it.

a. high fidelity
b. monophonic
c. stereophonic
d. antenna

REVIEW and EXTENSION 36

tacks
sole
soar
weave

insult
convict
suspect
extract

empire
umpire
medal
metal

onion
trillion
wrestle
treasure

duel
dial
poet
diet

SOUNDS and PATTERNS

1. Say each word below. Write the list word that is a homophone of each word.

a. sore **b.** tax **c.** soul **d.** we've

2. Read the sentences in the box. The italicized words are homographs.

Homographs
We shall *record* all the songs the chorus sings.
That old *record* sounds very scratchy.

Write the homographs for the respellings below.

(kon′ vikt, kən vikt′) (sə spekt′, sus′ pekt)
(in′ sult, in sult′) (ek strakt′, eks′ trakt)

3. Read each of the following sentences carefully. One letter is missing from the italicized word in each sentence. Write each italicized word correctly.

a. Jill received a *me_al* for good sportsmanship.
b. Copper is a *me_al*.
c. My *di_t* does not include ham.
d. An *_mpire* may include many nations.
e. An *_mpire* rules on the plays in the game.

4. In which words is /yən/ spelled *ion* as in *million*?

5. Answer each question below with a list word.

a. Which word rhymes with *measure*?
b. Which word begins with /r/?

6. Write the list word for each meaning below.

a. a fight between two persons
b. a disk that turns, as on a telephone
c. a person who writes poetry

DICTIONARY

1. Study the entries at the right. Write the words that you would not syllabicate at the end of a line of writing.

2. Write the form of each word in parentheses that correctly completes the paragraph.

The cottage is not in (accept) condition. It is (sore) in need of repair.

3. Write the numeral that tells which entry for *sole* is derived from the Latin *solus* (alone).

4. Which entry word has more than one stressed syllable? Draw a curved line under the letters that have primary stress.

5. Write *adj.* or *v.* to tell the use of the word *perfect* in each sentence.

a. We enjoyed perfect weather for swimming.

b. Kim worked hard to perfect her art.

CHECK POINT

If you misspelled words in Units 31–35, decide why you made errors. Study those words again. Then study the new words.

ac cept (ak sept′), *v.* To consent to receive; to take when given. **—acceptable,** *adj.* 1. Worth accepting. 2. Satisfactory. **—acceptance,** *n.* The taking of something offered or given.

per fect (*adj.* pėr′ fikt; *v.* pər fekt′), *adj.* Without fault; having absolutely nothing wrong. **—***v.* To make faultless; to improve something until it is perfect. **—perfection,** *n.* State of being perfect.

soar (sôr, sōr), *v.* To fly gracefully; to sail upward.

sole[1] (sōl), *n.* 1. The under surface of the foot. 2. The bottom of a shoe or boot. **—***v.* To furnish with a sole. Have your shoes *soled.* [From Latin *solea* shoe from Latin *solum* bottom.]

sole[2] (sōl), *n.* A flatfish that has a small mouth, small fins, and small eyes set close together. [From Latin *solea* the solefish.]

sole[3] (sōl), *adj.* Single; only; one. I was the *sole* heir to the fortune. [From Latin *solus* alone.]

sore (sôr, sōr), *adj.* 1. Hurting; causing pain. 2. Irritated. **—sorely,** *adv.* Badly.

sta tion ar y (stā′ shə ner′ ē), *adj.* 1. Permanent. 2. Not moving; staying in one place. [From Latin *statio* standing still.]

umpire's
union's
graduates'
graduates
associate's
associates
principal's
aviators'
poets
accepted
excepted
expected
honorable
honorably
sensible
adaptable
perfection
conviction
appreciation

WORD STRUCTURE

1. Which three list words are plurals?

2. Read the phrases in the box. Notice the difference in the spellings of the singular possessives and the plural possessives.

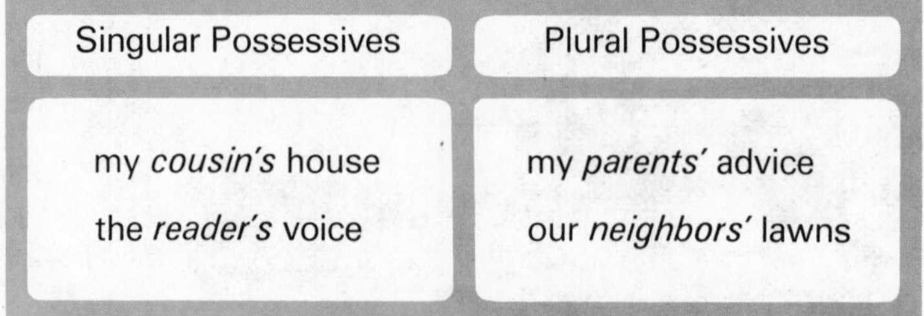

Singular Possessives	Plural Possessives
my *cousin's* house	my *parents'* advice
the *reader's* voice	our *neighbors'* lawns

Write the list word that is the correct form of the word in parentheses. After each word, write *s.* or *pl.* to show which possessive form you have written.

a. the (principal) rule **b.** an (umpire) ruling
c. the (graduate) robes **d.** the (union) request
e. his (associate) letter **f.** two (aviator) caps

3. Write the list word for each meaning below.

a. left out **b.** consented **c.** counted on

4. Compare the spelling of each base word in the box with its derived form.

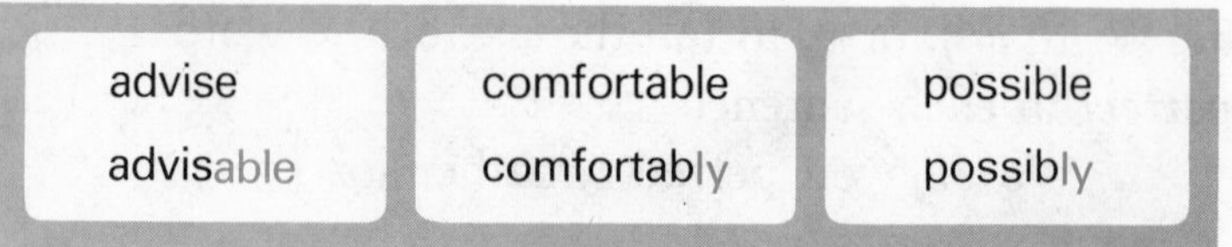

advise	comfortable	possible
advisable	comfortably	possibly

Write a derived form of each word in parentheses.

a. (honor) discharge **b.** (honor) settled
c. (adapt) arrangement **d.** (sense) decision

5. Write the *ion* form of each word below.

a. convict **b.** appreciate **c.** perfect

PROGRESS CHECK

Be sure you can spell all the words in the first lists from Units 31–36.

ON YOUR OWN

1. Complete the puzzle.

Across

1. painful
3. thought
6. toll or duty
7. result
8. valuable things

Down

1. not crooked
2. get away
4. formal fight
5. region

1			2	■	3	4		5
	■	■		■	■		■	
	■	■		■	■		■	
	■	6			■		■	
	■	■		■	■	■	■	■
	■	■	7					
	■	■	■	■	■	■	■	■
8								■

2. Write the word that belongs with each group.

a. teacher, ____, superintendent
b. freshman, sophomore, ____

3. Write each italicized word. Draw a curved line under the letters in the stressed syllable.

a. *object* of art **b.** to *object*
c. to *conduct* **d.** bad *conduct*

4. Write the homophone that should be used in place of each word in parentheses.

a. We slept in a comfortable (birth).
b. The (manner) was built high on a hill.
c. The (night) was very courageous.
d. The huge boat was tied to the (peer).

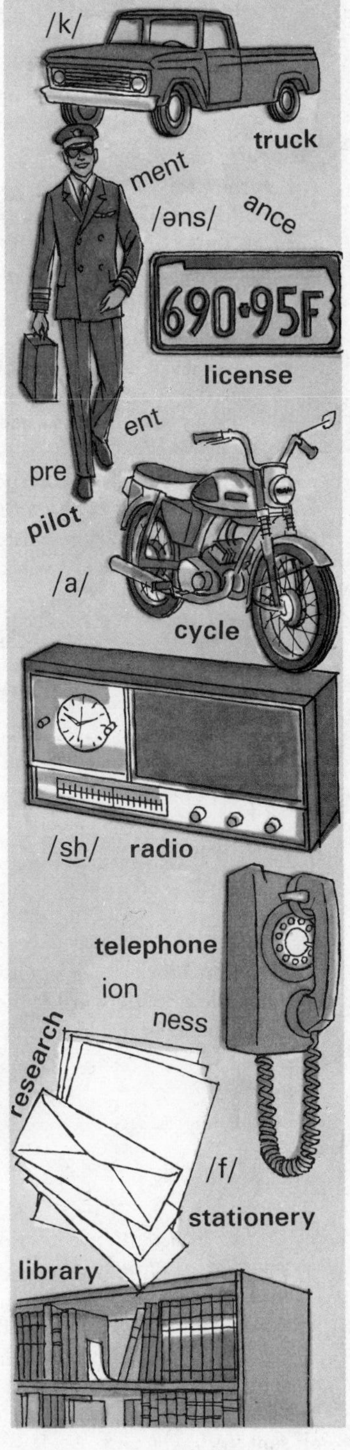

SPELLING DICTIONARY

KEY TO PRONUNCIATION

a	hat, cap	i	it, pin	ou	house, out	zh	measure, seizure
ā	age, face	ī	ice, five	sh	she, rush	ə	represents:
ã	care, air	ng	long, bring	th	thin, both		a in about
ä	father, far	o	hot, rock	ᴛʜ	then, smooth		e in taken
ch	child, much	ō	open, go	u	cup, butter		i in pencil
e	let, best	ô	order, all	u̇	full, put		o in lemon
ē	equal, see	oi	oil, voice	ü	rule, move		u in circus
ėr	term, learn						

Notice the phonetic spellings of *manufacture* in the sample entries below. In these respellings, each sound in *manufacture* is represented by a different symbol. The respelling symbols used in this dictionary are listed above. Notice that some of the symbols are made up of two letters; others have marks over a single letter.

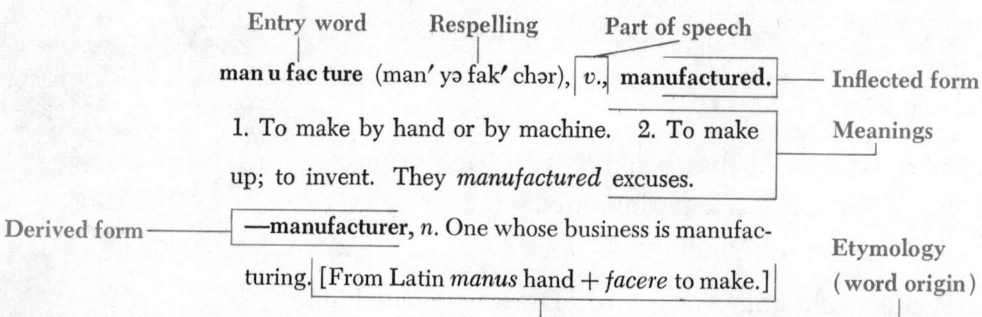

Entry word
Respelling
Part of speech
man u fac ture (man′ yə fak′ chər), *v.*, **manufactured.**
Inflected form
1. To make by hand or by machine. 2. To make up; to invent. They *manufactured* excuses.
Meanings
Derived form
—manufacturer, *n.* One whose business is manufacturing. [From Latin *manus* hand + *facere* to make.]
Etymology (word origin)

Guide Words. The guide words at the top of each dictionary page will help you locate words. The first guide word is the same as the first entry word on that page. The second guide word is the same as the last entry word on the page.

a-
account

A

a-, *prefix.* In a certain condition or manner, as in *ashamed* or *afire.*

-able, *adj. suffix.* 1. Worthy of. 2. Able to.

a broad (ə brôd′), *adv.* Outside one's own country. They traveled *abroad* last summer.

ab sence (ab′ səns), *n.* Being away; the state of being absent.

ab sent (*adj.* ab′ sənt; *v.* ab sent′), *adj.* Not present; missing. —*v.* Keep away.

a bun dant (ə bun′ dənt), *adj.* Plentiful; having a large amount. —*Ant.* **scarce.**

ac cept (ak sept′), *v.* To consent to receive; to take when given. **—acceptable,** *adj.* 1. Worth accepting. 2. Satisfactory. **—acceptance,** *n.* The taking of something offered or given.

ac cord ing (ə kôr′ ding), *adj.* Agreeing. **—according to,** *prep.* As stated by.

ac count (ə kount′), *n.* 1. Money kept in a bank. 2. A record of money spent and received. 3. A report or explanation. —*v.* To explain.

ac cu rate (ak′ yər it), *adj.* Careful and exact; having no errors. —*Syn.* **correct.**

ache (āk), *n.* A dull pain. —*v.* To hurt with a dull pain; to throb.

a cous tics (ə küs′ tiks, -kous′-), *n.* 1. The science of sound. 2. Everything that has to do with the way sound is produced and heard in a certain building.

ac quaint (ə kwānt′), *v.* To make known.

a cre (ā′ kər), *n.* A unit of measure for land; 160 square rods.

ac tion (ak′ shən), *n.* An act; something that is done.

a dapt (ə dapt′), *v.* To make fit a new situation.

ad journ (ə jėrn′), *v.* To end a meeting.

a dopt (ə dopt′), *v.* 1. To accept formally. 2. To take a child as one's own. **—adoption,** *n.* The formal acceptance.

ad van tage (ad van′ tij, -vän′-), *n.* A favorable condition. What are the *advantages* of air travel? **—advantageous,** *adj.* Favorable.

ad ven ture (ad ven′ chər), *n.* An exciting experience. **—adventurous,** *adj.* Liking adventure; bold. [From Latin *ad* to + *venire* to come.]

ad vice (ad vīs′), *n.* A suggestion as to how one should act; a recommendation.

ad vise (ad vīz′), *v.* 1. To inform. 2. To tell someone how to behave. **—advisable,** *adj.* Wise; sensible.

ad vo cate (*n.* ad′ və kit; *v.* ad′ və kāt), *n.* 1. A person who argues for a cause. 2. In some countries, a lawyer. —*v.* To speak in favor of. We do not *advocate* the use of force in training the puppies.

af ford (ə fôrd′), *v.* 1. To have enough money for. 2. To give. The fort *affords* protection.

af ter ward (af′ tər wərd, äf′-), *adv.* In the time following.

ag ate (ag′ it), *n.* A precious stone with stripes or bands of varying colors.

-age, *n. suffix.* Result of.

a gent (ā′ jənt), *n.* A person who acts for another.

ag gres sion (ə gresh′ ən), *n.* An attack; a hostile act.

aisle (īl), *n.* A passageway between seats in a church, theater, or auditorium.

al tar (ôl′ tər), *n.* A table set in the most important place in a church.

al ter (ôl′ tər), *v.* To change; to make different.

al ter nate (*v.* ôl′ tər nāt; *adj.* ôl′ tər nit), *v.* To take turns; to go first one way and then another. —*adj.* 1. Another. A detour is an *alternate* route to a destination. 2. First one, then the other. The cloth has *alternate* stripes.

al to (al′ tō), *n., pl.* **altos.** The part in music sung by the second highest singing voice.

a mount (ə mount′), *n.* Quantity; how much there is of something.

am phib i an (am fib′ ē ən), *n.* 1. A plant or animal that can live on land or in water. 2. A plane that can take off and land on either land or water. [From Greek *amphi* of both kinds + *bios* life.]

am pli fi er (am′ plə fī′ ər), *n.* An apparatus that increases the strength of an electric current.

-ance, *n. suffix.* Being.

an cient (ān′ shənt), *adj.* Very old.

an gel (ān′ jəl), *n.* A spirit; a being often pictured as having wings and having light around its head.

an gle (ang′ gəl), *n.* 1. A figure formed by two lines coming together. 2. Point of view.

an gry (ang′ grē), *adj.* Filled with anger.

an kle (ang′ kəl), *n.* The joint between the foot and the leg.

an noy (ə noi′), *v.* To trouble; to disturb.

an nu al ly (an′ yủ ə lē), *adv.* Once a year. [From Latin *annus* year.] —*Syn.* **yearly.**

-ant, *n. suffix.* Person who acts or thing that acts, as *assistant* or *irritant.*

anx ious (angk′ shəs, ang′-), *adj.* Feeling fear or anxiety. **—anxiously,** *adv.* In a fearful way.

ap pa ra tus (ap′ ə rā′ təs, -rat′ əs), *n.* Special equipment; instruments for a particular use.

ap ply (ə plī′), *v.,* **applied.** 1. To ask for, especially to ask for work. 2. To put to use.

ap point (ə point′), *v.* 1. To decide on; to set a time for. 2. To name a person to do a job. **—appointment,** *n.* An engagement.

ap pre ci ate (ə prē′ shē āt), *v.* Be grateful for. **—appreciation,** *n.* Thanks. [From Latin *appretiare* to value.]

ap pro pri ate (*adj.* ə prō′ prē it; *v.* ə prō′ prē āt), *adj.* Fitting; suitable. —*v.* 1. To set aside. Congress *appropriates* money for foreign aid. 2. To take without permission.

Pronunciation Key: **hat, āge, cãre, fär; let, ēqual, tėrm; it, īce; hot, ōpen, ôrder; oil, out; cup, pủt, rüle; child; long; she; thin; ᴛʜen; zh,** measure; **ə** represents **a** in about, **e** in taken, **i** in pencil, **o** in lemon, **u** in circus.

ar bor[1] (är′ bər), *n.* A shady place formed by trees or shrubs; an orchard. [From Latin *herba* grass.]

ar bor[2] (är′ bər), *n.* The main shaft of a machine which transmits force to other moving parts. [From Latin *arbor* a tree.]

ar chi tec ture (är′ kə tek′ chər), *n.* 1. The designing of structures. 2. The style of buildings.

ar e a (ãr′ ē ə), *n.* 1. An amount of surface. The *area* of the floor is 600 square feet. 2. Region or district. The northwest *area* of the United States is mountainous.

ar mor (är′ mər), *n.* A protective covering of leather or metal worn by medieval soldiers.

ar my (är′ mē), *n., pl.* **armies.** A large body of people trained for war.

ar range (ə rānj′), *v.* To put in order. —**arrangement,** *n.* The act or result of putting in order.

ar rive (ə rīv′), *v.,* **arrives, arriving, arrived.** To come to.

ar se nal (är′ sə nəl), *n.* A place for storing weapons and ammunition.

ar ti cle (är′ tə kəl), *n.* 1. Object; thing. 2. A writing on a special subject. 3. In English, the articles are *a, an,* and *the.*

ar ti fi cial (är′ tə fish′ əl), *adj.* 1. Unreal; not genuine. The jewels are *artificial.* 2. Made by humans. Lake Mead near Hoover Dam is an *artificial* lake.

a shamed (ə shāmd′), *adj.* Feeling shame.

a side (ə sīd′), *adv.* Toward one side.

as sem bly (ə sem′ blē), *n., pl.* **assemblies.** 1. A gathering of people. The Constitution guarantees the right of *assembly.* 2. Putting together. The *assembly* of the toy is explained on the box.

as sign ment (ə sīn′ mənt), *n.* The work a person or group of persons is responsible for carrying out; that which is assigned.

as so ci ate (*v.* ə sō′ shē āt; *n.* ə sō′ shē it), *v.* To link together in our thinking. We *associate* writing with an author. —*n.* A person or thing connected with another. —**association,** *n.* Group of people joined together for some purpose; a club.

as so ci a tive (ə sō′ shē ā′ tiv), *adj.* In mathematics, involving a number of terms and having results not dependent on how the terms are grouped.

as tound (ə stound′), *v.* To surprise; to amaze.

at tach (ə tach′), *v.* To fasten; to join. —**attachment,** *n.* Affection; a feeling of fondness.

at tend (ə tend′), *v.* 1. To be present at. 2. To pay attention to; to take care of.

at ten tion (ə ten′ shən), *n.* The state of noting and considering. Please give me your *attention.*

at tic (at′ ik), *n.* The space in a building just below the roof; a garret.

at trac tion (ə trak′ shən), *n.* The power of arousing interest. I was the center of *attraction.*

at trac tive (ə trak′ tiv), *adj.* Charming; pleasing. —**attractively,** *adv.* In a pleasing way.

au di ence (ô′ dē əns), *n.* A group that listens to a performance. [From Latin *audire* to hear.]

au di o-vis u al (ô′ dē ō vizh′ ů əl), *adj.* Having to do with both hearing and seeing. [From Latin *audire* to hear + *videre* to see.]

au di to ri um (ô′ də tôr′ ē əm, ô′ də tōr′ ē əm), *n.* A place for an audience; a room, hall, or building where people sit to see and hear a play, movie, concert, etc. [From Latin *audire* to hear.]

au thor (ô′ thər), *n.* A person who writes stories, plays, articles, etc.

a vi a tor (ā′ vē ā′ tər, av′ ē ā′ tər) *n.* The pilot of an airplane.

a void (ə void′), *v.* To keep away from.

a wake (ə wāk′), *v.,* **awoke** or **awaked, awaking.** To wake up; to arouse.

a woke (ə wōk′), *v., past* of **awake.** Cliff *awoke* early this morning.

ax is (ak′ sis), *n., pl.* **axes.** A real or imaginary straight line around which something rotates. The axle is the *axis* of a wheel.

B

bal ance (bal′ əns), *n.* An instrument for weighing. —*v.,* **balanced, balancing.** To distribute weight evenly.

bal co ny (bal′ kə nē), *n.* A projecting platform outside or inside a building.

bal sa (bôl′ sə, bäl′-), *n.* A tree, grown in tropical climates, that has strong, lightweight wood.

ban dit (ban′ dit), *n.* One who steals or kills in a merciless way; an outlaw.

ban quet (bang′ kwit), *n.* A large meal attended by many people. —*Syn.* **feast.**

bar rel (bar′ əl), *n.* 1. A large, round container used for storing liquids. 2. The metal tube of a gun.

ba sin (bā′ sən), *n.* 1. A shallow bowl used for washing. 2. All of the land drained by a river.

ba sis (bā′ sis), *n.* The foundation; that on which something is based.

bay ou (bī′ ü, -ō), *n.* A marshy body of water in southern United States.

bead (bēd), *n.* A small, round stone or other ornamental material that may be strung on a necklace, sewn on cloth, etc.

berth (bėrth), *n.* 1. A space reserved for a ship to anchor. 2. A place to sleep, especially on a train or ship.

be tray (bi trā′), *v.* 1. To help the enemies of one's country. 2. To give away a secret.

bi an nu al ly (bī an′ yu̇ ə lē), *adv.* Twice a year. [From Latin *bi* twice + *annus* year.]

bil lion (bil′ yən), *n.* One thousand million.

bi sect (bī sekt′, bī′,-), *v.* To cut into two equal parts.

blame (blām), *v.* To find fault with.

blank (blangk), *adj.* Having an empty space, often meant to be filled in with writing. —*Syn.* **empty.**

blare (blãr), *v.* To make a loud, harsh sound. —*n.* A loud, harsh sound like that of a trumpet.

bom bard (*v.* bom bärd′; *n.* bom′ bärd), *v.* To attack with heavy firing of weapons. —*n.* A medieval weapon that threw great stones.

book keep er (bu̇k′ kē′ pər), *n.* A person whose job is keeping records of business matters.

bor der (bôr′ dər), *n.* 1. A line between two countries. 2. Edge. 3. Margin.

both er (boᴛʜ′ ər), *v.* To trouble; to annoy.

boul der (bōl′ dər), *n.* A large rock.

bounce (bouns), *v.* To bound or rebound like a ball; to spring back.

bound[1] (bound), *v., past* and *past part.* of **bind.** Bales of hay are *bound* with wire. —*adj.* Certain; sure. We are *bound* to find the answer. [From Old English *bounden.*]

bound[2] (bound), *v.* To leap; jump. —*n.* A leap or spring upward. [From French *bondir* leap.]

bound[3] (bound), *adj.* On the way; going to; determined to. They were *bound* for home. [From Middle English *boun* ready.]

bound[4] (bound), *n.* A boundary line, as of a piece of property. [From Latin *bodina* a bound, limit.]

brack et (brak′ it), *n.* 1. One of a pair of marks used in writing, such as [ ]. 2. A fixture on a wall for holding a shelf, lamp, etc.

brake (brāk), *n.* Something to slow down or stop a car or other vehicle.

buck et (buk′ it), *n.* A pail.

bu gle (byü′ gəl), *n.* A musical instrument similar to a trumpet and made of brass. [From Latin *buculus* ox.]

bump (bump), *v.* To hit; to run against.

buoy ant (boi′ ənt, bü′ yənt), *adj.* 1. Energetic and happy. 2. Able to float.

bur y (ber′ ē), *v.,* **buried.** To put in earth; to cover with earth or other things.

bush el (bu̇sh′ əl), *n.* A measure for fruit or vegetables, equal to 32 quarts.

busi ness (biz′ nis), *n.* Way of making money; trade; occupation.

C

ca nar y (kə nãr′ ē), *n.* A small singing bird, usually yellow.

can cel (kan′ səl), *v.* 1. To cross out; to remove. 2. To call off. The game was *canceled* because of rain.

can ner y (kan′ ər ē), *n.* A factory in which foods are canned.

cap size (kap sīz′, kap′ sīz), *v.* To turn bottom side up; to upset.

cap ture (kap′ chər), *v.* 1. To seize and keep an animal by force. 2. To take a person prisoner. [From Latin *capere* to seize.]

car ol (kar′ əl), *n.* A Christmas song.

car pen ter (kär′ pən tər), *n.* A person who builds things, mainly of wood. [From Latin *carpentarius* carriage maker, from *carpentum* wagon.]

car riage (kar′ ij), *n.* 1. A horse-drawn cart for carrying people. 2. A cart made especially for carrying babies.

car toon (kär tün′), *n.* 1. An amusing drawing. 2. A motion picture made from drawings.

cash (kash), *n.* Money that is readily exchangeable.

cas u al (kazh′ u̇ əl), *adj.* 1. Informal; natural; easy. 2. Not according to a plan; happening by chance. [From Latin *casus* chance.]

cat a logue or **cat a log** (kat′ ə lôg, -log), *n.* A complete list of all the items for sale, all the books in a library, etc.

---

ca tal pa (kə tal′ pə), *n.* A tree with broad leaves, large flowers, and pods.

ceil ing (sē′ ling), *n.* 1. The inside top covering of a room. 2. The height of clouds above the earth.

ce ment (sə ment′), *n.* A substance that hardens after being mixed with water.

cer tain (sėr′ tən), *adj.* 1. One particular, but unnamed. There was a castle in a *certain* country. 2. Sure. —*Ant.* **unsure; uncertain.** —**certainly,** *adv.* Surely; definitely.

cer tif i cate (sər tif′ ə kit), *n.* An official paper proving something about a person named in it. Do you have a birth *certificate?*

chalk board (chôk′ bôrd′, -bōrd′), *n.* A hard material with a smooth surface, used in writing with chalk.

cham pi on (cham′ pē ən), *n.* A person who has won a contest.

chap el (chap′ əl), *n.* A small church; a small place of worship.

chap ter (chap′ tər), *n.* A main division of a book, usually beginning on a new page.

charge (chärj), *n.* 1. A person or thing under the care of another. 2. Responsibility; duty. 3. Care. 4. The price; expense. 5. Attack. —*v.* 1. To write down as a debt. 2. To accuse.

char ter (chär′ tər), *n.* A written grant giving the right to organize a colony, business, etc.

chase (chās), *v.*, **chased, chasing.** To run after in order to catch. [From Old French *chacier* chase.]

cheap (chēp), *adj.*, **cheaper, cheapest.** Costing little money; inexpensive.

cheer ful (chir′ fəl), *adj.* Happy, full of cheer.

chef (shef), *n.* A cook; a head cook in a restaurant. [From Old French *chef* chief.]

choir (kwīr), *n.* A group of singers.

choose (chüz), *v.*, **chose, chosen.** To decide upon; to select.

cho ral (kôr′ əl), *adj.* Having to do with a chorus or choir.

chord (kôrd), *n.* A combination of harmonious musical notes sounded together.

cho rus (kôr′ əs, kōr′-), *n.* A group of singers, often a large group.

chose (chōz), *v.*, *past* of **choose.** The team *chose* a new captain.

cir cu lar (sėr′ kyə lər), *adj.* In the shape of a circle.

cir cum fer ence (sər kum′ fər əns), *n.* The distance around a circle or sphere.

cit i zen (sit′ ə zən, -sən), *n.* A person who by birth or by choice is a member of a nation or state. [From Old French *cite* city.]

civ il (siv′ əl), *adj.* Polite. —*Ant.* **impolite.**

civ i li za tion (siv′ ə lə zā′ shən), *n.* 1. The state of being civilized; not being savage. 2. The way people live in a particular time and place. [From Latin *civis* citizen.]

claim (klām), *v.* 1. To demand as one's right. The United States *claims* part of Antarctica. 2. To state. They *claim* they saw robbers.

clev er (klev′ ər), *adj.* Skillful; intelligent. —**cleverness,** *n.* Being clever; showing intelligence. —**cleverly,** *adv.* In a clever way.

cli mate (klī′ mit), *n.* The year-round weather of an area.

clum sy (klum′ zē), *adj.* Not moving easily; unskillful. —*Syn.* **awkward.**

co ax i al (kō ak′ sē əl), *adj.* 1. With a common axis. 2. Having to do with a cable made of small cables wound around a central core or axis.

cof fee (kôf′ ē, kof′-), *n.* A drink made from ground coffee beans.

col i se um (kol′ ə sē′ əm), *n.* A large building or outdoor stadium with seats for people who watch games and sports.

col lec tion (kə lek′ shən), *n.* A group of objects; a number of objects kept together.

col lege (kol′ ij), *n.* A place of learning for students who have completed high school.

com-, *prefix.* With; together.

com e dy (kom′ ə dē), *n.* An amusing play with a happy ending. —*Ant.* **tragedy.**

com fort a ble (kumf′ tə bəl, kum′ fər-), *adj.* Feeling comfort; feeling at ease.

com i cal (kom′ ə kəl), *adj.* Funny.

com mu ni ca tion (kə myü′ nə kā′ shən), *n.* Means of passing on information or ideas to those nearby or far away. [From Latin *communis* common.]

com mu ni ty (kə myü′ nə tē), *n.* People living in the same locality under the same government; people with the same interests.

com mu ta tive (kə myü′ tə tiv), *adj.* In mathematics, describing an operation consisting of one or more steps with the result not depending on the order of the steps.

com pel (kəm pel′), *v.*, **compelled.** To force; to make someone do something. [From Latin *com* with + *pellere* to drive.]

com pete (kəm pēt′), *v.* To try to win a contest.

com pose (kəm pōz′), *v.* 1. To write music or literary works; to put together any work of art. 2. To calm. *Compose* yourself. [From Latin *com* together + French *poser* to place.]

com press (*v.* kəm pres′; *n.* kom′ pres), *v.* To press something together so that it takes up less space. —*n.* A cloth that is held firmly over a wound or over an inflamed part of the body. [From Latin *com* with + *premere* to press.]

con-, *prefix.* With; together.

con di tion (kən dish′ ən), *n.* 1. Circumstance; state of affairs. 2. Something that one agrees to do before something else occurs.

con duct (*v.* kən dukt′; *n.* kon′ dukt), *v.* 1. To lead. 2. To behave. *Conduct* yourself in a dignified manner. 3. To carry out. I am *conducting* the country's foreign affairs. —*n.* Behavior.

con fine (*v.* kən fīn′; *n.* kon′ fīn), *v.* To restrict; to restrain; to keep within limits. —*n.* Border; limit. We could not leave the *confines* of the prison.

con flict (*n.* kon′ flikt; *v.* kən flikt′), *n.* A fight; a clash of opinions. —*v.* To disagree sharply. That version of the story *conflicts* with mine.

con fuse (kən fyüz′), *v.* To bring into disorder; to make a person unable to think clearly.

con gress (kong′ gris), *n.* The highest lawmaking body of a nation; when capitalized, the lawmaking body of the United States.

con ser va tion (kon′ sər vā′ shən), *n.* Keeping; saving; not changing or destroying.

con sid er (kən sid′ ər), *v.* 1. To think over; to think about. 2. To think of others in a helpful way.

con so nant (kon′ sə nənt), *n.* A speech sound made by closing part of the passageway of the breath; any letter that stands for these speech sounds.

con ti nent (kon′ tə nənt), *n.* One of the great land areas of the world.

con tin ue (kən tin′ yü), *v.* To go on with; to keep on; to proceed. —*Ant.* **discontinue.**

con tract (*n.* kon′ trakt; *v.* kən trakt′), *n.* An agreement, often a written one. —*v.* 1. To enter into agreement. We *contracted* to buy by the month. 2. To become smaller. The pupil of the eye expands and *contracts.*

con trast (*v.* kən trast′; *n.* kon′ trast), *v.* To discriminate; to compare so as to show differences. —*n.* Difference, often a great or striking one.

con trol (kən trōl′), *v.*, **controlled, controlling.** To restrain; to have power over.

con ven tion (kən ven′ shən), *n.* A formal meeting for people with a special purpose in common. [From Latin *com* together + *venire* to come.]

con ver sa tion (kon′ vər sā′ shən), *n.* Talk; exchange of ideas, news, or opinions by word of mouth.

con vict (*v.* kən vikt′; *n.* kon′ vikt), *v.* To find guilty of a crime; to find guilty of wrongdoing of any kind. —*n.* A prisoner; a person convicted of a crime.

cor sage (kôr säzh′), *n.* Flowers arranged to be worn.

cos tume (*n.* kos′ tüm, -tyüm; *v.* kos tüm′, -tyüm′), *n.* Clothing; clothing worn during a certain period of time; clothing worn on stage or at a fancy dress ball. —*v.* To put on special clothing; to design special clothing.

coun cil (koun′ səl), *n.* A meeting held to discuss or to advise; the people who hold the meeting. [From Latin *concilium* call together.]

coun sel (koun′ səl), *v.* To advise; to recommend a course of action. The teacher *counseled* us to study. [From Latin *consulere* to consult.]

coun try side (kun′ trē sīd′), *n.* The country as contrasted with the city.

cour age (kėr′ ij), *n.* Bravery. —*Ant.* **cowardice.** —**courageous,** *adj.* Full of courage; brave.

court (kôrt, kōrt), *n.* 1. A place marked for a game. 2. A place where a judge presides and legal decisions are made. 3. The residence of a ruler. —*v.* To persuade a person to marry; to seek.

cour te ous (kėr′ tē əs), *adj.* Polite; having good manners. [From Old French *cort* a court.]

cour te sy (kėr′ tə sē), *n.* 1. Politeness. 2. A kind act. 3. Gift. The flowers in the auditorium are through the *courtesy* of the florist. —*Ant.* **rudeness.**

cow ard (kou′ ərd), *n.* A person who has no courage; a person who runs from danger.

cow ard ice (kou′ ər dis), *n.* Fearfulness; being without courage.

PRONUNCIATION KEY: **hat, āge, cãre, fär; let, ēqual, tėrm; it, īce; hot, ōpen, ôrder; oil, out; cup, pu̇t, rüle; child; long; she; thin; ᴛʜen; zh,** measure; **ə** represents **a** in about, **e** in taken, **i** in pencil, **o** in lemon, **u** in circus.

coy (koi), *adj.* 1. Shy. 2. Pretending to be shy.

crate (krāt), *n.* A box, usually with a wooden frame, used for transporting goods.

crev ice (krev′ is), *n.* A crack.

cru el (krü′ əl), *adj.* Unkind; giving pain. **—cruelty,** *n.* The state of being cruel.

crus ta cean (krus tā′ shən), *n.* A water animal with a jointed body covered with a shell. A lobster is a *crustacean.* [From Latin *crusta* shell.]

crys tal (kris′ təl), *n.* A piece of glass, ice, or other clear substance.

cu cum ber (kyü′ kum bər), *n.* A green, gourdlike vegetable used in salads and for pickles.

cur few (kėr′ fyü), *n.* A ringing of a bell at a fixed time very evening as a signal, usually for children to come in off the streets. [From French *couvrir* to cover + *feu* fire.]

cur rent (kėr′ ənt), *n.* 1. A body of air, water, or similar substance flowing in a particular direction. 2. A flowing of electricity. [From Latin *currere* to run.]

cur tain (kėr′ tən), *n.* A covering for a window, doorway, or stage.

cush ion (ku̇sh′ ən), *n.* A cloth stuffed with soft material.

cus tard (kus′ tərd), *n.* A baked or boiled pudding made of eggs, sugar, milk, etc.

cute (kyüt), *adj.,* **cuter, cutest.** Attractive, in a dainty or pretty way.

cut ler y (kut′ lər ē), *n.* Knives and other instruments for cutting.

cy cle (sī′ kəl), *n.* A series of events that repeat themselves, each time in the same order. The cocoon is one phase in the life *cycle* of the butterfly.

cyl in der (sil′ ən dər), *n.* Any long, round object with flat, circular bases.

D

dai ly (dā′ lē), *adv.* Every day; once a day.

dan ger ous (dān′ jər əs), *adj.* Full of risk; unsafe.

dar ling (där′ ling), *n.* A person very dear to another; a favorite. *—adj.* Very dear; much loved.

dash (dash), *v.* 1. To run suddenly. 2. A short line.

dawn (dôn), *n.* The break of day; the first sunlight in the morning.

de-, *prefix.* Down; from.

deaf (def), *adj.* 1. Not able to hear; not able to hear well. 2. Not willing to hear; heedless.

deal (dēl), *v.* 1. To carry on business. 2. To distribute. **—dealer,** *n.* One who deals in something. I am a car *dealer.*

dec o rate (dek′ ə rāt), *v.,* **decorating, decorates, decorated.** To trim.

dec o rat ed (dek′ ə rā′ tid), *v., past* of **decorate.** *—adj.* Ornamented; trimmed; adorned.

de crease (di krēs′), *v.* To grow less; to make something become less. [From Latin *de* down + *crescere* to grow.]

deed (dēd), *n.* 1. An act. 2. A document.

de lay (di lā′), *v.* To make late; to cause to be slower.

de light (di līt′), *v.* To please greatly. **—delightful,** *adj.* Very pleasing.

de light ed (di lī′ tid), *v., past* of **delight.** *—adj.* Greatly pleased; joyful; glad.

de liv er (di liv′ ər), *v.* 1. To set free. 2. To bring.

de liv er y (di liv′ ər ē, -liv′ rē), *n.* The act of bringing.

dense (dens), *adj.* Packed together tightly. [From Latin *densus* dense.] *—Syn.* **thick.**

den tist (den′ tist), *n.* A person whose business is to care for teeth.

de pend a ble (di pen′ də bəl), *adj.* Reliable; trustworthy.

de pend ence (di pen′ dəns), *n.* 1. Reliance on another for support or help. 2. Trust.

de pend ent (di pen′ dənt), *adj.* 1. Relying on another for support or help. A child is *dependent* on his or her parents. 2. Controlled or influenced by something else. Good crops are *dependent* on having the right kind of weather.

de pot (dē′ pō), *n.* A railroad or bus station.

de scend (di send′), *v.* To go or come down. [From Latin *de* down + *scandere* to climb.]

de scribe (di skrīb′), *v.* To give a picture of something in words. [From Latin *de* down + *scribere* to write.]

de scrip tion (di skrip′ shən), *n.* An account that describes; an account that gives a picture of something in words. **—descriptive,** *adj.* Having to do with words that give pictures.

de sire (di zīr′), *v.* To want; to wish for.

des sert (di zėrt′), *n.* Food, often sweet, served at the end of a meal.

di al (dī′ əl), *n.* A disk that can be turned, as a telephone *dial.*

dic tion ar y (dik′ shə ner′ ē), *n., pl.* **dictionaries.** A book with an alphabetical arrangement of words giving meanings and other information.

di et (dī′ ət), *v.* 1. To eat special or limited amounts of food and drink. 2. To eat food; feed. —*n.* The usual food and drink for a person or animal.

dif fer ence (dif′ ər əns, dif′ rəns), *n.* 1. The state of not being the same. 2. In arithmetic, the result obtained by subtracting.

dif fer ent (dif′ ər ənt, dif′ rənt), *adj.* Not alike; not the same.

dif fi cult (dif′ ə kult, -kəlt), *adj.* Hard to do; requiring much effort or trouble. —*Ant.* **easy.**

di men sion (də men′ shən), *n.* A measurement of length, breadth, or thickness. The board's *dimensions* are 2 in. × 4 in. × 6 ft. [From Latin *dis* out + *metiri* to measure.]

dim ple (dim′ pəl), *n.* A small hollow on a human face; a natural indentation.

di rec tion (də rek′ shən, dī-), *n.* 1. A rule for doing or making something. 2. The line in which something is moving or facing. 3. That which a compass shows.

di rec to ry (də rek′ tər ē, dī-, -trē), *n.* An alphabetical list of people's names, as a telephone *directory*.

dis-, *prefix.* 1. Not. 2. Away from. 3. Opposite of.

dis a gree (dis′ ə grē′), *v.* To fail to agree. —*Ant.* **agree.**

dis card (*v.* dis kärd′; *n.* dis′ kärd), *v.* To throw away. —*n.* Anything that is thrown away.

dis charge (*v.* dis chärj′; *n.* dis chärj′, dis′ chärj), *v.* 1. To let go; dismiss. 2. To shoot a gun. 3. To give off or let out. The river *discharges* into a lake. —*n.* A release; a dismissal; a letting go.

dis re spect (dis′ ri spekt′), *n.* Lack of respect; the feeling or showing of a low opinion. —*Ant.* **respect.**

dis tance (dis′ təns), *n.* The space between two things.

dis tant (dis′ tənt), *adj.* Being far apart or far away.

dis trib u tive (dis trib′ yə tiv), *adj.* In mathematics, describing an operation upon each part with a result that is equal to that obtained by operating on the whole.

dive (dīv), *v.* To plunge downward; to go headfirst into water.

di vi sion (də vizh′ ən), *n.* 1. In arithmetic, the process of finding how many times one number is contained in another. 2. An army unit usually made up of five battle groups.

doc ile (dos′ əl), *adj.* Easily trained or managed. —*Syn.* **obedient.**

do mes ti cate (də mes′ tə kāt), *v.* To change from wild to tame. [From Latin *domus* house.]

do min ion (də min′ yən), *n.* 1. One of the states within the British Commonwealth. 2. Power.

dour (dür, dour), *adj.* Unpleasant; gloomy; stern.

draft (draft, dräft), *n.* 1. A current of air. 2. The selecting of people to serve in an army. 3. A plan; a sketch. I made three different *drafts* of my speech.

du el (dü′ əl, dyü′-), *n.* A fight between two persons, usually with formal rules.

du et (dü et′), *n.* A piece of music performed by two persons or instruments. [From Latin *duo* two.]

dump ling (dump′ ling), *n.* 1. A rounded piece of boiled or steamed dough usually served with meat. 2. A kind of dessert made by enclosing fruit in a piece of dough and baking or steaming it.

E

ear nest (ėr′ nist), *adj.* Very serious in purpose. —*Ant.* **insincere.** —**earnestly,** *adv.* In a serious way.

earth quake (ėrth′ kwāk′), *n.* A trembling or shaking of the earth caused by movements in its crust.

eas i ly (ē′ zə lē), *adv.* In a way that is without effort.

ed u ca tion (ej′ u̇ kā′ shən), *n.* The act of being educated; learning; acquiring formal knowledge. I lacked an *education.*

ef fect (ə fekt′), *n.* That which is caused. One *effect* of the snowstorm was the closing of school.

ef fort (ef′ ərt), *n.* The making of an attempt; the use of strength of mind or body.

e lec tion (i lek′ shən), *n.* The process of choosing a person for office by voting.

Pronunciation Key: **hat, āge, cãre, fär; let, ēqual, tėrm; it, īce; hot, ōpen, ôrder; oil, out; cup, pu̇t, rüle; child; long; she; thin; ꟻHen; zh,** measure; **ə** represents **a** in about, **e** in taken, **i** in pencil, **o** in lemon, **u** in circus.

el e ments (el′ ə mənts), *n. pl.* 1. The weather; bad weather. Wild animals must seek protection from the *elements.* 2. Distinct varieties of matter. Iron and copper are *elements.*

else (els), *adj.* Other; different; instead. Would you like to buy something *else?*

em broi der y (em broi′ dər ē, -broi′ drē), *n.* The art of sewing a raised pattern into cloth.

em pire (em′ pīr), *n.* A territory, usually large, ruled by one person or one nation.

em ploy (em ploi′), *v.* To hire; to give paid work to. **—employment,** *n.* Paid work.

-ence, *n. suffix.* The act of; the state of.

en coun ter (en koun′ tər), *n.* 1. A meeting; an unexpected meeting. 2. A meeting of enemies; a fight; a battle.

en er gy (en′ ər jē), *n.* Power; the capacity of people, machines, etc., to accomplish work. **—energetic,** *adj.* Active.

en force (en fôrs′, -fōrs′), *v.* To make by force; to make effective.

en gi neer (en′ jə nir′), *n.* 1. A person in charge of a railroad train. 2. A person trained in one of the branches of engineering.

en list (en list′), *v.* 1. To ask the support of. 2. To join a cause, as the armed services. *—Syn.* **engage.**

e nough (i nuf′), *adj.* All that is needed.

-ent, *n. suffix.* Person who acts or thing that acts, as *president* or *absorbent.*

en vi ron ment (en vī′ rən mənt), *n.* Surroundings; everything that surrounds or influences a living thing.

e quip (i kwip′), *v.,* **equipped, equipping.** To fit out; to give the necessary tools, resources, clothing, etc. This zoo is not *equipped* to handle elephants. **—equipment,** *n.* The tools, machinery, etc., necessary for a particular activity.

-er[1], *adj.* or *adv. suffix.* Used for comparative forms. More.

-er[2], *n. suffix.* A person who; that which.

es cape (es kāp′), *v.* To get away by flight, hiding, etc. **—escapism,** *n.* Habitual avoidance of unpleasant things.

es pe cial ly (es pesh′ ə lē, -pesh′ lē), *adv.* Particularly; in a special way; exclusively.

-est, *adj.* or *adv. suffix.* Used for superlative forms. Most.

es tu ar y (es′ chů er′ ē), *n.* 1. An arm of the sea where the tide meets the river's current. 2. An inlet of the sea.

etc., *abbr.* of **et cetera.** And so forth. [From Latin *et* and + *cetera* other things.]

ex-, *prefix.* 1. Out; from. 2. Former; earlier.

ex act ly (eg zakt′ lē), *adv.* In an accurate way; precisely.

ex am i na tion (eg zam′ ə nā′ shən), *n.* 1. A test to determine what a student has learned. 2. An investigation; the process of studying, as a doctor's *examination* of a patient.

ex am ple (eg zam′ pəl, -zäm′-), *n.* 1. A brief problem for a student to solve. 2. A particular case that is used to represent many similar cases.

ex cel lent (ek′ sə lənt), *adj.* Very good.

ex cept (ek sept′), *prep.* Not including; not counting. **—exception,** *n.* One that is excepted or something that is taken out from others.

ex change (eks chānj′), *v.* To give or replace one thing for another.

ex cite ment (ek sīt′ mənt), *n.* Being excited; being stirred emotionally.

ex cuse (*v.* ek skyüz′; *n.* ek skyüs′), *v.* To forgive; to pardon. *—n.* That which one gives as a reason or an explanation.

ex hib it (eg zib′ it), *v.* To put on show. [From Latin *ex* out + *habere* to have.] *—Syn.* **display.**

ex pect (ek spekt′), *v.* To think likely to happen. **—expectation,** *n.* A state of expecting.

ex pen sive (ek spen′ siv), *adv.* Costly; costing much money. *—Ant.* **inexpensive.**

ex pe ri ence (ek spir′ ē əns), *n.* Anything one has taken part in or lived through.

ex per i ment (*n.* ek sper′ ə mənt; *v.* ek sper′ ə-ment), *n.* Trial; a test to discover something. *—v.* To try out; to test.

ex pert (*n.* eks′ pėrt; *adj.* ek spėrt′, eks′ pėrt), *n.* One who has special skill or knowledge; a specialist. *—adj.* Having special skill or knowledge. **—expertly,** *adv.* Skillfully.

ex port (*v.* ek spôrt′, -spōrt′; *n.* eks′ pôrt, -pōrt), *v.* To ship to another country. *—n.* Something shipped to another country.

ex pres sion (ek spresh′ ən), *n.* Showing feelings or meanings by words, looks, gestures, etc. [From Latin *ex* out + *pressum* pressed.]

ex tra (eks′ trə), *adj.* Beyond what is used or needed; additional. *—Syn.* **spare.**

ex tract (*v.* ek strakt′; *n.* eks′ trakt), *v.* 1. To draw forth; to pull out. The dentist *extracted* a tooth. 2. To separate. Apple juice is *extracted* from apples. *—n.* A concentration of a substance. Beef *extract* is used in gravies.

F

fac to ry (fak′ tər ē, fak′ trē), *n., pl.* **factories.** A manufacturing plant; a building in which things are made. [From Latin *facere* to make.]

fault (fôlt), *n.* 1. An error; a mistake. 2. A cause for blame.

fa vor (fā′ vər), *n.* 1. Kind assistance; help. 2. A state of being liked or approved. I am out of *favor.* **—favorable,** *adj.* Being in favor of. **—favorite,** *adj.* Most liked; chosen above others; favored.

fea ture (fē′ chər), *n.* 1. A long movie. 2. A quality that stands out.

fel low (fel′ ō, -ə), *n.* A person, man, or boy.

fer ry (fer′ ē), *v.* To carry people and vehicles across short distances of water.

fes ti val (fes′ tə vəl), *n.* A time of celebration.

feu dal (fyü′ dəl), *adj.* Having to do with the civilization of the Middle Ages. —*Ant.* **democratic. —feudalism,** *n.* The social and political system of Europe in the Middle Ages.

fe ver (fē′ vər), *n.* A body temperature higher than normal. **—feverish,** *adj.* Having a fever.

fig ure (fig′ yər), *v.* 1. To think; to try to understand. 2. To calculate; to work with numbers. —*n.* 1. Symbol for a number, such as 1, 2, 3, etc. 2. Shape, such as a square, triangle, cube, etc.

file[1] (fīl), *n.* 1. A cabinet in which papers are kept. 2. A line of persons, animals, or things one behind another. —*v.* 1. To put away papers, etc., in order. Please *file* those letters. 2. To march or move in file. [Partly from Middle French *file* row, and Latin *filum* a thread.]

file[2] (fīl), *n.* A steel tool with a rough surface for smoothing hard substances. —*v.* To smooth or wear away with a file. [From Old English *feol.*]

fi nal ly (fī′ nə lē), *adv.* In the end; at last.

fiord (fyôrd, fyōrd), *n.* An inlet of the sea between high cliffs, especially in Norway.

fis sion (fish′ ən), *n.* The process of breaking into parts, especially the splitting of an atom.

flare (flãr), *v.* 1. To flame up briefly or unsteadily. 2. To spread out in the shape of a bell. This skirt *flares* at the bottom. 3. To signal by lights. The rockets *flared* a warning. —*n.* 1. A bright, unsteady light that lasts only a short time. 2. A part that spreads out.

flat car (flat′ kär′), *n.* A railroad car without sides or roof.

flaw (flô), *n.* An imperfection; a defect.

flint (flint), *n.* A very hard stone from which early humans made primitive tools.

flown (flōn), *v., past part.* of **fly.** The birds had *flown* south.

flur ry (flėr′ ē), *n.* A sudden, brief shower of snow, rain, or wind.

folks (fōks), *n.* People; friends; relatives.

force (fôrs, fōrs), *n.* 1. A body of armed soldiers. 2. Any body of people trained for a special job. 3. Energy; strength; power.

for est er (fôr′ ə stər, for′-), *n.* A person in charge of a forest.

for est ry (fôr′ ə strē, for′-), *n.* The science of planting and caring for forests.

for gave (fər gāv′), *v., past* of **forgive.** I *forgave* them for telling the secret.

for give (fər giv′), *v.,* **forgave, forgiven, forgiving.** To pardon; to excuse.

fort (fôrt, fōrt), *n.* A military stronghold; a building or group of buildings made so that they can be defended from attack.

forth (fôrth, fōrth), *adv.* On; onward; forward.

for tune (fôr′ chən), *n.* 1. Luck. 2. Good luck. 3. Great wealth.

for ward (fôr′ wərd), *adv.* Onward; toward the front; toward the future. —*Ant.* **backward.**

fought (fôt), *v., past* of **fight.** Our team *fought* for the championship.

foun tain (foun′ tən), *n.* A stream of water that rises in the air by natural or artificial means.

frag ment (frag′ mənt), *n.* A piece; a part broken from the whole. —*Ant.* **whole.**

freight (frāt), *n.* Cargo; goods carried by train, ship, truck, or plane. The *freight* can be shipped tomorrow.

-ful, *adj. suffix.* Full of; having the qualities of.

fu ner al (fyü′ nər əl, fyün′ rəl), *n.* A service or ritual for a person who has died.

fun gus (fung′ gəs), *n.* A parasitic plant; a plant that lives on other living things.

fu ri ous (fyu̇r′ ē əs), *adj.* Very angry.

fur nace (fėr′ nis), *n.* An enclosed structure to hold a very hot fire.

Pronunciation Key: **hat, āge, cãre, fär; let, ēqual, tėrm; it, īce; hot, ōpen, ôrder; oil, out; cup, pu̇t, rüle; child; long; she; thin;** ᴛʜen; **zh,** measure; **ə** represents **a** in about, **e** in taken, **i** in pencil, **o** in lemon, **u** in circus.

fur nish (fėr′ nish), *v.* 1. To provide with furniture. 2. To provide what is needed; to supply. The school does not *furnish* all books. [From French *fournir* to complete; furnish. Doublet of FURNITURE.]

fur ther (fėr′ ᴛʜər), *compar. adj.* and *adv.*, *superl.* **furthest.** 1. A greater distance. 2. More; in addition. May I help you *further*?

fu tile (fyü′ təl), *adj.* Useless; not worthwhile. **—futility,** *n.* 1. Uselessness. 2. Unimportance.

fu ture (fyü′ chər), *n.* The time that is yet to come; the time following the present. —*Ant.* **past.**

G

gadg et (gaj′ it), *n.* A small device; a small part of a machine.

gain (gān), *v.* To get; to come to have; to earn.

ga rage (gə räzh′, -räj′), *n.* 1. A building to house a car. 2. A repair shop for cars.

gar bage (gär′ bij), *n.* Waste matter; trash; matter that has been thrown away.

gar ment (gär′ mənt), *n.* An article of clothing.

gar net (gär′ nit), *n.* A dark-red gem.

gem (jem), *n.* A precious stone; a jewel.

gen u ine (jen′ yu̇ ən), *adj.* Real; true.

gey ser (gī′ zər, -sər), *n.* A spring that sends hot water and steam from the earth.

gla cier (glā′ shər), *n.* A permanent mass of snow that forms wherever more snow falls in winter than can melt in summer.

glide (glīd), *v.* To sail smoothly; to move smoothly.

glimpse (glimps), *n.* A quick look; a brief view of something.

gloom y (glü′ mē), *adj.* Dark; sad; dismal.

golf (golf, gôlf), *n.* A game, played with clubs, whose object is to hit a small ball into each of the holes on a golf course.

good ness (gu̇d′ nis), *n.* The state of being good.

gov ern ment (guv′ ərn mənt, -ər-), *n.* The process of ruling a country.

gov er nor (guv′ ər nər, guv′ nər), *n.* 1. The highest executive official in state government. 2. A person in charge of governing a colony, etc.

grad u ate (*v.* graj′ u̇ āt; *n., adj.* graj′ u̇ it), *v.* To receive a diploma or certificate stating that one has completed a school, a college, a course, etc. —*n.* A person who has completed grade school, high school, college, or any course of study. —*adj.* Having to do with completion of a certain school, a course, etc. **—graduation,** *n.* The act or ceremony of graduating.

grain (grān), *n.* 1. The seed of cereal grass, such as wheat, corn, and oats. 2. The direction of fibers in wood. 3. A speck; a tiny particle.

gram mar (gram′ ər), *n.* The study of how words are related to each other; the rules of relating words to each other.

graph ite (graf′ īt), *n.* A soft carbon material used in making pencils.

great ly (grāt′ lē), *adv.* Very; in a great manner.

grief (grēf), *n.* Sadness; sorrow.

grieve (grēv), *v.* To feel very sad; to mourn.

guard (gärd), *n.* A person who keeps watch; a person who keeps something or someone safe. —*v.* To keep watch over.

guest (gest), *n.* A person invited to share a meal, to stay in someone's home, or to be otherwise entertained.

guide (gīd), *v.* To lead; to direct.

guild (gild), *n.* During the Middle Ages, an organization of people all doing the same kind of work.

gym na si um (jim nā′ zē əm), *n.* A large room for indoor sports, in some regions referred to as **gym.**

gy ro scope (jī′ rə skōp), *n.* A wheel mounted so its axis can turn. *Gyroscopes* keep ships balanced.

H

hang ar (hang′ ər, -gər), *n.* A building in which airplanes are kept and serviced.

hap pi ness (hap′ ē nis), *n.* The state of being happy; gladness.

har dy (här′ dē), *adj.* 1. Strong; able to bear discomfort and hardship. 2. Of a plant, able to withstand cold.

head ache (hed′ āk′), *n.* A pain inside the head.

head quar ters (hed′ kwôr′ terz), *n.* The main or central office.

heart y (här′ tē), *adj.* 1. Friendly; unrestrained. 2. Abundant. We ate a *hearty* meal.

heav en (hev′ ən), *n.* The space that surrounds the earth; the firmament.

hem i sphere (hem′ ə sfir), *n.* 1. One half of a sphere. 2. One half of the earth's surface.

her self (hėr self′), *pron.* Used to refer to a noun or *she* in order to make a statement more emphatic.

high school (hī′ skül′), *n.* The school attended after eighth grade or junior high school.

high way (hī′ wā′), *n.* A public road; a main road.

hike (hīk), *n.* A long walk taken for pleasure or exercise.

hoarse (hôrs, hōrs), *adj.* Sounding harsh; not smooth in sound; low and husky.

hon est (on′ ist), *adj.* Truthful; not deceitful.

hon or (on′ ər), *v.* To respect; to show great regard for. —*n.* 1. Privilege. 2. Glory; fame.

how ev er (hou ev′ ər), *adv.* Nevertheless; yet.

hu man (hyü′ mən), *adj.* Belonging to or having to do with people.

hun gry (hung′ grē), *adj.* Feeling hunger.

hur ri cane (hėr′ ə kān), *n.* A tropical storm with violent winds and usually heavy rain.

hy dro foil (hī′ drə foil), *n.* 1. A fin just below the water line of a boat that raises the boat out of the water at high speeds. 2. A watercraft that has such a fin. [From Greek *hydor* water.]

hy dro plane (hī′ drə plān), *n.* A swift, light motorboat that glides on the water's surface. [From Greek *hydor* water.]

hy giene (hī′ jēn), *n.* A system of rules for healthful living.

I

-ible, *adj. suffix.* 1. Worthy of. 2. Tending to. 3. Able to.

-ic, *adj. suffix.* 1. Being. 2. Relating to. 3. Like that of.

i ci cle (ī′ si kəl), *n.* Ice formed by the freezing of dripping water.

i de a (ī dē′ ə), *n.* A thought; a notion.

ig no rant (ig′ nər ənt), *adj.* Being without knowledge; knowing nothing.

i mag ine (i maj′ ən), *v.* To create a mental image; to form an idea. —*Syn.* **pretend.** **—imagination,** *n.* The process of imagining; the act of creating a mental image; the ability to imagine.

im me di ate ly (i mē′ dē it lē), *adv.* Instantly; without delay.

im por tance (im pôr′ təns), *n.* The state of being important; significance; being of value.

im pos si ble (im pos′ ə bəl), *adj.* Not possible; incapable of being done. —*Ant.* **possible.**

im prop er (im prop′ ər), *adj.* Not right; not correct; not in good taste. —*Ant.* **proper.**

im prove (im prüv′), *v.* To make better; to become better. **—improvement,** *n.* Being improved; being better.

in-, im-, ir-, or **il-,** *prefix.* Not.

in cor rect (in′ kə rekt′), *adj.* Not correct; improper; wrong. —*Ant.* **correct.**

in crease (in krēs′), *v.* To become more; to cause to become more. [From Latin *in* in + *crescere* to grow.]

in de pend ent (in′ di pen′ dənt), *adj.* 1. Not controlled by others. 2. Not requiring something else; not needing other people.

in dus try (in′ də strē, -dus′ trē), *n.* 1. Business. 2. Work; steady attention to a task.

in ex pen sive (in′ ik spen′ siv), *adj.* Not costly; cheap.

in fir ma ry (in fėr′ mər ē), *n.* 1. A hospital. 2. The part of a building used for the care of the sick.

in for ma tion (in′ fər mā′ shən), *n.* Knowledge received from others.

in hab it ant (in hab′ ə tənt), *n.* A person who lives in a place.

in quire (in kwīr′), *v.* To try to find out by questions; to ask.

in stance (in′ stəns), *n.* An example.

in stant (in′ stənt), *n.* A very brief period of time; moment.

in stru ment (in′ strə mənt), *n.* 1. Something other than the voice used to produce music. 2. Means. 3. Tool; implement. Doctors use medical *instruments.* [From Latin *instruere* to instruct + *mentum.*]

in sult (*v.* in sult′; *n.* in′ sult), *v.* To treat with scorn; to speak scornfully to. —*n.* An act or speech that expresses scorn of someone.

inter-, *prefix.* Between; among.

in ter est (in′ tər ist, -trist), *v.* To attract the attention of; to cause someone to be concerned.

in ter est ed (in′ tər ə stid, -trə-; -tə res′-), *v., past* of **interest.** —*adj.* Feeling or showing interest, sympathy, or curiosity. —*Ant.* **disinterested.**

PRONUNCIATION KEY: **hat, āge, cãre, fär; let, ēqual, tėrm; it, īce; hot, ōpen, ôrder; oil, out; cup, pu̇t, rüle; child; long; she; thin; ᴛʜen; zh,** measure; **ə** represents **a** in about, **e** in taken, **i** in pencil, **o** in lemon, **u** in circus.

in ter mis sion (in′ tər mish′ ən), *n.* The time between two parts of a play or show. [From Latin *inter* between + *mittere* to send.] —*Syn.* **pause; recess.**

in ter na tion al (in′ tər nash′ ə nəl, -nash′ nəl), *adj.* Existing between or among nations.

in ter plan e tar y (in′ tər plan′ ə ter′ ē), *adj.* Existing or operating between planets.

in ter state (in′ tər stāt′, in′ tər stāt′), *adj.* Between or among states.

i ris (ī′ ris), *n.* 1. A plant that grows from a bulb and has brightly colored flowers. 2. The colored part of the eye.

is land (ī′ lənd), *n.* Land surrounded by water.

-ism, *n. suffix.* 1. Act of. 2. State of. 3. Theory of.

isth mus (is′ məs), *n.* A strip of land connecting two larger bodies of land.

-ity, *n. suffix.* Condition or quality of being.

-ive, *adj. suffix.* Tending to.

J

jade (jād), *n.* A stone that is usually green and is used for decoration.

jail or (British) **gaol** (jāl), *n.* A prison; a place in which people are confined.

jan i tor (jan′ ə tər), *n.* One who takes care of an apartment or other building. [From Latin *janitor* doorkeeper, from *janua* door.]

jas per (jas′ pər), *n.* A gem that may be one of various colors —brown, white, red, or yellow.

jew el (jü′ əl), *n.* A precious stone; a stone that has been cut and polished and is used as an ornament.

jour nal (jėr′ nəl), *n.* 1. A magazine. 2. A newspaper. 3. A diary. [From Latin *diurnus* daily. Doublet of JOURNEY.]

jour ney (jėr′ nē), *n.* A trip. [From Latin *diurnus* daily. Doublet of JOURNAL.]

ju bi lee (jü′ bə lē), *n.* A time of joy; a festive occasion. —*Syn.* **celebration.**

jun ior (jün′ yər), *adj., abbr.* **Jr.** 1. A name to distinguish a son from a father with the same first name. 2. Younger. 3. Having to do with the third year in high school or college.

ju ry (jür′ ē), *n., pl.* **juries.** A body of people selected to give a judgment in a legal matter.

jus tice (jus′ tis), *n.* 1. Being just or fair. 2. The giving of the rewards or punishments that are deserved.

K

keen (kēn), *adj.* 1. Sharp. 2. Eager; enthusiastic.

kin der gar ten (kin′ dər gär′ tən), *n.* A class in school that children attend before the first grade. [From German *kinder* children + *garten* garden.]

kind ness (kīnd′ nis), *n.* 1. The state of being kind. 2. A kind act.

knight (nīt), *n.* 1. During the Middle Ages, a soldier on horseback. 2. A person to whom a king or queen has given the rank of knight. **—knightly,** *adj.* Like a knight.

knowl edge (nol′ ij), *n.* Knowing; understanding; learning.

L

la bor (lā′ bər), *n.* Work; toil. —*v.* To work; to toil. **—laborer,** *n.* One who toils, often at physical work. [From Latin *labor* work.]

lace (lās), *n.* 1. An open weaving or net of fine thread in an ornamental pattern. 2. A cord, string, etc., for pulling or holding something together.

lack (lak), *n.* A want; a need that is not met. —*v.* To be without; to be wanting.

lau rel (lôr′ əl, lor′-), *n.* Shrub or tree; bay tree.

law yer (lô′ yər), *n.* A person who advises about the law; an attorney.

league (lēg), *n.* 1. An association, a club, or a society. 2. A measure of distance, about three miles.

least (lēst), *superl. adj.* The smallest; the smallest amount.

-less, *adj. suffix.* Not having; without.

let tuce (let′ is), *n.* A plant used in salads.

li brar y (lī′ brer ē, -brər-), *n., pl.* **libraries.** A building holding a collection of books. [From Latin *liber* book.]

li cense (lī′ səns), *n.* A right granted by law; a paper showing a specific right a person has earned. [From Latin *licere* to be permitted.]

life guard (līf′ gärd), *n.* A person who watches swimmers to prevent accidents in water and to rescue drowning swimmers.

loaf[1] (lōf), *n., pl.* **loaves.** 1. Bread shaped and baked in one piece. 2. Anything like a loaf in shape. [From Old English *half* loaf, bread.]

loaf[2] (lōf), *v.* To spend time idly; do nothing. [Origin uncertain.]

lone ly (lōn′ lē), *adj.* Being without company.

lone some (lōn′ səm), *adj.* Being sad because of lack of company.

lum ber men (lum′ bər mən), *n. pl.* People who cut and prepare timber.

lu nar (lü′ nər), *adj.* Having to do with the moon.

-ly, *adv. suffix.* In a certain way.

M

ma chine (mə shēn′), *n.* A device consisting of fixed and moving parts.

mag a zine (mag′ ə zēn′, mag′-), *n.* 1. A publication that appears regularly. 2. The place where cartridges are put in an automatic gun.

mag ni fy (mag′ nə fī), *v.* To cause to look larger.

main (mān), *adj.* Chief; principal. **—mainly,** *adv.* Chiefly.

mam mal (mam′ əl), *n.* Any of the animals that give milk to their young.

man or (man′ ər), *n.* 1. A feudal estate. 2. The main house on any large estate.

man's[1], *contraction.* Man is.

man's[2], *possessive.* Of a man, or person.

man tel (man′ təl), *n.* A shelf above a fireplace.

man tle (man′ təl), *n.* 1. A long, loose cloak. 2. Any covering.

man u fac ture (man′ yə fak′ chər), *v.,* **manufactured.** 1. To make by hand or by machine. 2. To make up; to invent. They *manufactured* excuses. **—manufacturer,** *n.* A person whose business is manufacturing. [From Latin *manus* hand + *facere* to make.]

mar i time (mar′ ə tīm), *adj.* Related to the sea. [From Latin *mare* the sea.]

mar quee (mär kē′), *n.* A structure over a theater entrance; a covered entrance.

mar riage (mar′ ij), *n.* State of being joined as husband and wife.

mar ry (mar′ ē), *v.,* **marries, marrying, married.** To wed.

ma te ri al (mə tir′ ē əl), *n.* 1. Cloth; fabric. 2. The substance from which a thing is made. *—adj.* 1. Being of importance in a legal case. 2. Made of matter; not spiritual.

meant (ment), *v., past* of **mean.** I *meant* it.

meas ure (mezh′ ər, mā′ zhər), *v.,* **measured, measuring.** To find the size, volume, length, etc. *—n.* 1. The act of finding the size, volume, etc., of something. 2. A bar of music. 3. A course of action. **—measurement,** *n.* The result of measuring.

med al (med′ əl), *n.* A flat piece of metal with words or designs, given as an award.

med i cine (med′ ə sən), *n.* A drug or other substance used to cure sickness.

mem ber (mem′ bər), *n.* A person who belongs to a club, community, or other group. [From Latin *membrum* part.]

mem o ry (mem′ ər ē, mem′ rē), *n., pl.* **memories.** The ability to remember; what one remembers. [From French *memoir.*]

men ace (men′ is), *n.* A threat; a nuisance.

-ment, *n. suffix.* The act of; a state of.

men tion (men′ shən), *v.* To refer to; to speak of.

men u (men′ yü, mā′ nyü), *n.* A list of the food served at one meal. [From French *menu* small, detailed.]

met al (met′ əl), *n.* A substance, such as iron, silver, gold, or copper, that conducts heat and electricity and is often shiny.

mez za nine (mez′ ə nēn), *n.* A small balcony in a theater. *—Syn.* **gallery.**

mid night (mid′ nīt′), *n.* Twelve o'clock at night, when one day ends and a new day begins.

mil lion (mil′ yən), *n.* One thousand thousand.

min er al o gy (min′ ə ral′ ə jē, -rol′-), *n.* The science of studying minerals. **—mineralogist,** *n.* One engaged in the study of minerals.

min is ter (min′ ə stər), *n.* 1. A cleric serving a church. 2. A person who is given charge of a department of the government. *—v.* To attend to comfort or wants; to be of service.

mint[1] (mint), *n.* 1. Any of a group of fragrant plants often used for flavoring. 2. A piece of candy flavored with mint.

mint[2] (mint), *n.* A place where money is coined by public authority. *—v.* To coin money.

mis-, *prefix.* 1. Wrong; wrongly. 2. Bad; badly.

mis sion (mish′ ən), *n.* 1. An assignment. 2. Persons sent to accomplish a special task. [From Latin *mittere* to send.]

mis spell (mis spel′), *v.* To spell wrongly.

PRONUNCIATION KEY: **h**a**t**, **ā**g**e**, **c**ã**re**, **f**ä**r**; **let**, **ē**q**ual**, **tėrm**; **it**, **īce**; **hot**, **ōpen**, **ôrder**; **oil**, **out**; **cup**, **pu̇t**, **rüle**; **child**; **long**; **she**; **thin**; **ᴛʜen**; **zh,** measure; **ə** represents **a** in about, **e** in taken, **i** in pencil, **o** in lemon, **u** in circus.

mis take (mis tāk′), *v.* To misunderstand. —*n.* An error; blunder.

mis un der stand (mis′ un dər stand′), *v.* To understand wrongly; to fail to understand.

mod es ty (mod′ ə stē), *n.* Humbleness; freedom from vanity. —*Ant.* **boastfulness.**

mol lusk (mol′ əsk), *n.* An animal with a soft body, no backbone, and usually a shell. [From Latin *molluscus* soft.]

mo ment (mō′ mənt), *n.* An instant; a very brief period of time.

mor tar (môr′ tər), *n.* A mixture of sand, water, and cement that becomes stonelike when it dries. *Mortar* is used to hold bricks together.

mo tor (mō′ tər), *n.* 1. A device for changing electrical energy into mechanical energy. 2. An engine. [From Latin *movere* to move.]

mourn (môrn, mōrn), *v.* To feel or express deep sorrow or grief; to grieve. **—mourner,** *n.* One who mourns.

mov ie (mü′ vē), *n.* A motion picture; cinema.

mu se um (myü zē′ əm), *n.* A building where objects of art, science, or natural history are exhibited.

N

nar row (nar′ ō), *adj.* 1. Having little width; not wide. 2. Not large; not generous. 3. Barely possible. She had a *narrow* escape. —*v.* To lessen the width .

na tive (nā′ tiv), *adj.* Born in a specific place. Some Americans are *natives*, but others were born in other countries.

nec es sar y (nes′ ə ser′ ē), *adj.* Being needed; essential. **—necessarily,** *adv.* Because of necessity; because it must be.

ne ces si ty (nə ses′ ə tē), *n.* A thing that is needed; something one cannot do without.

neck (nek), *n.* 1. The part of the body that connects the head with the shoulders. 2. Any narrow part, such as the *neck* of a bottle.

neph ew (nef′ yü), *n.* The son of one's sister or brother.

nerv ous (nėr′ vəs), *adj.* 1. Having to do with nerves. 2. Being easily excited; not calm. **—nervousness,** *n.* Anxiety.

net work (net′ wėrk′), *n.* A group of radio or television stations.

news pa per (nüz′ pā′ pər, nyüz′-), *n.* Papers printed to report the news.

nour ish (nėr′ ish), *v.* To keep healthy with food; to feed; to keep alive. —*Syn.* **feed.** —*Ant.* **starve. —nourishment,** *n.* Food.

nug get (nug′ it), *n.* A lump of gold in its natural form.

O

o a sis (ō ā′ sis, ō′ ə-), *n.* A spot in the desert where there is water and therefore vegetation.

o bey (ō bā′), *v.* To do what one is told; to follow orders.

ob ject (*n.* ob′ jikt, -jekt; *v.* əb jekt′), *n.* 1. Thing; something that can be seen and touched. 2. A goal or purpose. What is the *object* of your experiment? —*v.* To be against; to make an objection; to dislike. **—objection,** *n.* A statement against; a reason for disliking.

o boe (ō′ bō), *n.* A woodwind instrument with a double reed and producing a high tone. [From French *hautbois* or *hautboy* high wood.]

ob serve (əb zėrv′), *v.* 1. To watch; to pay attention to. 2. To celebrate in a certain way. **—observance,** *n.* A following of a law or custom, as an *observance* of Independence Day.

oc cu py (ok′ yə pī), *v.*, **occupied.** 1. To fill; to take up a certain space. 2. Of an army, to live in enemy territory. 3. To be busy.

oc tet (ok tet′), *n.* Music performed by eight instruments or singers; a group of eight.

oc to pus (ok′ tə pəs), *n.* A sea animal with eight tentacles. [From Greek *okta* eight + *pous* foot.]

of fer (ôf′ ər, of′-), *v.* To present; to propose something so that it may be accepted.

one's[1], *contraction.* One is.

one's[2], *possessive.* Belonging to one.

on ion (un′ yən), *n.* A vegetable; the bulb of a plant with a strong smell and taste.

o pin ion (ə pin′ yən), *n.* One's personal views; a belief.

op po site (op′ ə zit), *adj.* As unlike as possible; as different in direction as possible.

-or, *n. suffix.* A person who; a thing that.

or chard (ôr′ chərd), *n.* Land on which fruit trees are grown; a fruit grove.

or ches tra (ôr′ kə strə), *n.* 1. A group of musicians who perform as a unit. 2. The main floor of a theater.

o rig i nal (ə rij′ ə nəl), *n.* 1. The first of its kind. 2. Able to make new things or behave in a new way. **—originally,** *adv.* In the beginning.

oth er wise (uᴛʜ′ ər wīz′), *adv.* In other ways.

ought (ôt), *v.* Should.

ounce (ouns), *n.* 1. A unit of weight, 1/16 of a pound avoirdupois. 2. A measure for liquids. In the United States, 16 ounces = 1 pint.

-ous, *adj. suffix.* Full of; having.

out line (out′ līn′), *n.* 1. A line around an object, showing only its shape. 2. A general plan.

out ra geous (out rā′ jəs), *adj.* Shocking; violent.

o ver due (ō′ vər dü′, -dyü′), *adj.* Due before this time; late; past due.

o ver joyed (ō′ vər joid′), *adj.* Very joyful.

own er (ō′ nər), *n.* A person who owns something.

oys ter (ois′ tər), *n.* A small shellfish used for food.

P

pain (pān), *n.* An ache; a feeling of suffering. **—painful,** *adj.* Hurting; causing suffering.

pal ace (pal′ is), *n.* 1. The official home of a king or queen. 2. Any very grand house.

pan el (pan′ əl), *n.* 1. A sunken or raised surface of a wall. 2. A small group of people having a discussion.

par a graph (par′ ə graf, -gräf), *n.* A group of sentences belonging together. [From Greek *para* beside + *graphein* to write.]

par don (pär′ dən), *n.* Forgiveness; the excusing of something.

par ent (pãr′ ənt), *n.* A father or mother.

pat tern (pat′ ərn), *n.* 1. Any arrangement of shapes and colors; a design. 2. A model in wood, paper, or words that is copied in making something.

pearl (pėrl), *n.* A white gem found inside the shells of oysters.

peas ant (pez′ ənt), *n.* A laborer who works the land in Europe, Asia, or South America.

ped al (ped′ əl), *n.* A lever operated by the foot.

ped dle (ped′ əl), *v.* To sell in small amounts.

peer[1] (pir), *n.* 1. A member of British nobility. 2. A person who is one's equal. [From Latin *par* equal.]

peer[2] (pir), *v.* To look closely in examining something. [From German *pliren* to peer.]

per cent (pər sent′), *n.* Hundredth.

per fect (*adj.* pėr′ fikt; *v.* pər fekt′), *adj.* Without fault; having absolutely nothing wrong. *—v.* To make faultless; to improve something until it is perfect. **—perfection,** *n.* State of being perfect.

per fume (*n.* pėr′ fyüm; *v.* pər fyüm′), *n.* 1. A substance used to give a pleasant smell. 2. A pleasant odor. *—v.* To give a pleasant odor to.

pe ri od (pir′ ē əd), *n.* 1. Span of time. 2. A point at the end of a sentence. **—periodical,** *n.* A magazine that is published at regular intervals.

per mis sion (pər mish′ ən), *n.* Consent.

phar ynx (far′ ingks), *n.* The tube that connects the mouth and passages of the nose to the esophagus.

pheas ant (fez′ ənt), *n.* A large, colorful game bird.

phys i cal (fiz′ ə kəl), *adj.* 1. Having to do with matter. 2. Having to do with the body rather than the mind.

pi a no (pē an′ ō), *n., pl.* **pianos.** A musical instrument with a keyboard.

pier (pir), *n.* A structure extending from land into water so that ships may dock to take on or discharge passengers or cargo.

pi lot (pī′ lət), *n.* 1. A person who operates an aircraft; an aviator. 2. A person who steers a boat into a harbor. *—v.* To guide; to steer.

plas ter (plas′ tər), *n.* A mixture of lime, sand, and water, used as a covering for walls.

pleas ure (plezh′ ər, plā′ zhər), *n.* A feeling of enjoyment; a good or pleasant feeling.

pli ers (plī′ ərz), *n.* A small tool shaped somewhat like scissors and used for turning nuts, twisting wires, etc.

P.M., *abbr.* Afternoon; between 12 o'clock noon and 12 o'clock midnight. [From Latin *post* after + *meridiem* noon.]

po et (pō′ it), *n.* A person who writes poetry.

po et ry (pō′ ə trē), *n.* Poems; verse. **—poetic,** *adj.* Having to do with poetry.

poise (poiz), *n.* Tact, graciousness.

poi son (poi′ zən), *n.* A harmful substance; anything that, when eaten, causes sickness or death. **—poisonous,** *adj.* Containing a substance harmful to life.

PRONUNCIATION KEY: **hat, āge, cãre, fär; let, ēqual, tėrm; it, īce; hot, ōpen, ôrder; oil, out; cup, pu̇t, rüle; child; long; she; thin; ᴛʜen; zh,** measure; **ə** represents **a** in about, **e** in taken, **i** in pencil, **o** in lemon, **u** in circus.

po lite (pə līt′), *adj.* Courteous; having good manners. **—politely,** *adv.* In a polite way.

po rous (pôr′ əs, pōr′-), *adj.* Full of holes; able to absorb liquids.

pos si ble (pos′ ə bəl), *adj.* Able to be done. **—possibly,** *adv.* Perhaps; it may be.

post-, *prefix.* After.

post pone (pōst pōn′), *v.* To put off until later. [From Latin *post* after + *ponere* to place.]

poul try (pōl′ trē), *n.* Fowl; domestic birds: chickens, turkeys, ducks, etc.

pour (pôr, pōr), *v.* To cause liquid to flow.

prac tice (prak′ tis), *n.* 1. Action done many times over for skill. 2. The business of a lawyer or doctor. **—***v.,* **practicing, practiced.** To work at; to do regularly. **—***Syn.* **drill; exercise.**

pre cise (pri sīs′), *adj.* Specific; exact.

prep a ra tion (prep′ ə rā′ shən), *n.* The act of getting ready.

press (pres), *n.* 1. Newspapers and magazines and the persons who write for them. 2. A clamping device for rackets, skis, etc. 3. A smooth and wrinkle-free condition (said of clothing). **—***v.* 1. To use force or weight steadily against; to push. 2. To iron clothes.

pres sure (presh′ ər), *n.* 1. A steady force. 2. The force, in pounds, exerted on each inch or other area. [From Latin *premere* to press.]

prey (prā), *n.* A victim; a hunted animal. **—***v.* To hunt and kill animals for food.

pri ma ry (prī′ mer′ ē, -mər-), *adj.* First in importance or time; main.

prim i tive (prim′ ə tiv), *adj.* 1. Uncivilized. 2. Having to do with very ancient times. 3. Very simple, as a *primitive* machine. [From Latin *primus* first.]

prin ci pal (prin′ sə pəl), *n.* The most important person; the head of a school or other institution. **—principally,** *adv.* Primarily.

prin ci ple (prin′ sə pəl), *n.* 1. A basic belief. 2. A rule of action. It is against my *principles* to lie. 3. A scientific explanation, as a *principle* of mathematics.

print (print), *v.* To make copies from type. **—printer,** *n.* One engaged in printing.

pri va cy (prī′ və sē), *n.* Being by oneself; being away from others.

pri vate (prī′ vit), *adj.* Not public; belonging to or used only by one person or by a few persons.

pro-, *prefix.* 1. Forward. 2. Out; forth. 3. In behalf of.

prob a bly (prob′ ə blē), *adv.* Very likely.

pro duce (*v.* prə düs′, -dyüs′; *n.* prod′ üs, prō′ düs), *v.,* **producing.** 1. To make; to bring forth. 2. To cause. 3. To bring a play to the public. **—***n.* What is brought forth or yielded on a farm. **—producer,** *n.* One who produces; one who makes. **—production,** *n.* The act of making.

pro gram (prō′ gram, -grəm), *n.* 1. A list of events. 2. The events in an entertainment. 3. A plan.

pro gress (*n.* prog′ res; *v.* prə gres′), *n.* A going forward; an improvement. **—***v.* To go forward; to improve.

pro hib it (prō hib′ it), *v.* To prevent by law or other means. The street sign *prohibits* turning left. **—***Syn.* **prevent.**

pro ject (*n.* proj′ ekt; *v.* prə jekt′), *n.* A plan; something that is undertaken. **—***v.* 1. To stick out. A peninsula *projects* into the sea. 2. To plan; to make a guess about the future on the basis of knowledge about the past.

prom ise (prom′ is), *n.* One's pledge to do something. **—***Syn.* **pledge; vow.**

proof (prüf), *n.* A way of showing the truth.

pro tec tion (prə tek′ shən), *n.* A shield against injury; the act of protecting. **—protective,** *adj.* Giving protection.

pro test (*n.* prō′ test; *v.* prə test′), *n.* An objection; an expression of dislike. **—***v.* To object; to express dislike or unwillingness.

prove (prüv), *v.* To show to be true.

P.S., *abbr.* Postscript; an addition to a letter, written after the signature. [From Latin *post* after + *scriptum* writing.]

pub lic (pub′ lik), *n.* The people in general; all the people of a town, country, etc. **—***adj.* Having to do with all the people; not private.

pud ding (pu̇d′ ing), *n.* A soft, sweet dessert.

Q

qual i fy (kwol′ ə fī), *v.,* **qualified.** To be eligible; to show oneself fit; to gain the right to participate.

quar rel (kwôr′ əl, kwor′-), *n.* An angry disagreement.

quar tet (kwôr tet′), *n.* Music performed by four instruments or four singers; a group of four.

qui et (kwī′ ət), *adj.* Still, without sound or motion. **—quietly,** *adv.* In a quiet way.

quilt (kwilt), *n.* A kind of blanket made of soft material between two layers of cloth.

quit (kwit), *v., past* **quit.** To stop. —*Syn.* **resign.**

R

ra cial (rā′ shəl), *adj.* Having to do with a race of people.

ra di a tion (rā′ dē ā′ shən), *n.* The giving off of rays of light, heat, etc. [From Latin *radius* ray.]

ra di a tor (rā′ dē ā′ tər), *n.* 1. A device used for heating. 2. Part of an automobile that contains water. [From Latin *radius* ray.]

ra di o (rā′ dē ō), *n., pl.* **radios** (short form of **radiotelegraphy**). A device for sending or receiving sound by electric waves without using wires.

ra di um (rā′ dē əm), *n.* A chemical element giving off certain rays, used in medicine and other ways. [From Latin *radius* ray.]

ra di us (rā′ dē əs), *n.* A straight line from the center to a point on a circle.

rail way (rāl′ wā′), *n.* A railroad.

rate (rāt), *n.* The amount of something measured in relation to something else.

re-, *prefix.* 1. Again. 2. Back.

re al ize (rē′ ə līz), *v.* To know fully and clearly.

reb el (*n.* reb′ əl; *v.* ri bel′), *n.* A person who fights against any kind of authority. —*v.* To fight against a law, a rule, or any authority. [From Latin *re* again + *bellum* war.]

re ceive (ri sēv′), *v.,* **receiving.** To be given.

rec i pe (res′ ə pē), *n.* Directions for preparing food.

rec tan gu lar (rek tang′ gyə lər), *adj.* Shaped like a rectangle; having four sides and four right angles.

re fer (ri fėr′), *v.,* **referred.** 1. To mention. 2. To relate; to have to do with. 3. To turn to for information. *Refer* to your dictionary. [From Latin *re* back + *ferre* to carry.]

re for est a tion (rē′ fôr ə stā′ shən, -for-), *n.* A planting of trees where they have been cut or destroyed.

re gards (ri gärdz′), *n. pl.* Good wishes.

re gret (ri gret′), *v.,* **regretted, regretting.** To feel sorry about.

reg u lar (reg′ yə lər), *adj.* 1. Usual. 2. According to rule. —*Ant.* **irregular.**

reign (rān), *n.* The period of time when a king or queen rules.

re li gion (ri lij′ ən), *n.* 1. Belief in God or gods. 2. A particular set of beliefs about God or gods.

re li gious (ri lij′ əs), *adj.* Having to do with religion.

re move (ri müv′), *v.* To take away.

re peat (ri pēt′), *v.* To say again; to do again.

re ply (ri plī′), *v.,* **replying, replied.** To answer.

re quest (ri kwest′), *v.* To ask for. [From Latin *re* back + *quaerere* to ask.]

re quire (ri kwīr′), *v.* To need; to think necessary. [From Latin *re* back + *quaerere* to ask.] —**requirement,** *n.* A need; what is required.

re search (ri sėrch′, rē′ sėrch), *n.* A careful study; a scientific investigation. —*v.* To search into.

re source (ri sôrs′, -sōrs′; rē′ sôrs, -sōrs), *n.* 1. A supply that fills a need. 2. Anything available.

re spect ful (ri spekt′ fəl), *adj.* Showing respect.

res pi ra tion (res′ pə rā′ shən), *n.* The act of breathing, taking in air and letting it out.

re view (ri vyü′), *v.* To look at or study again. [From Latin *re* again + *videre* to see.]

roast (rōst), *v.* To cook in an oven or over open fire. —**roaster,** *n.* A thing that roasts.

rock[1] (rok), *n.* 1. A stone. 2. Something firm like a rock. [From Old French *roque* rock.]

rock[2] (rok), *v.* To move back and forth. [From Old English *roccian* to rock, to shake.]

roll er (rō′ lər), *n.* Something that rolls, especially when used for crushing or smoothing.

rough (ruf), *adj.* 1. Bumpy; uneven. 2. Not polished. [From Old English *ruh.*] —*Ant.* **smooth.**

rou tine (rü tēn′), *n.* A repeating schedule; a method that does not vary.

S

sam ple (sam′ pəl, säm′-), *n.* One thing that shows what others of its kind are like; an example.

sat is fac to ry (sat′ is fak′ tər ē, -trē), *adj.* Good enough. —*Ant.* **unsatisfactory.**

sat is fy (sat′ is fī), *v.,* **satisfied.** To give enough to; to fill the needs of. —**satisfaction,** *n.* Feeling of contentment.

PRONUNCIATION KEY: **hat, āge, cãre, fär; let, ēqual, tėrm; it, īce; hot, ōpen, ôrder; oil, out; cup, pu̇t, rüle; child; long; she; thin; ᴛʜen; zh,** measure; **ə** represents **a** in about, **e** in taken, **i** in pencil, **o** in lemon, **u** in circus.

scarce (skārs), *adj.* Difficult to get; rare; in short supply. —**scarcely,** *adv.* Hardly.

scene (sēn), *n.* 1. A view; what can be seen. 2. The place, time, etc., of a story or drama.

scen er y (sē′ nər ē, sēn′ rē), *n.* 1. Landscape; scenes of a place, as country *scenery.* 2. The background on a stage.

scheme (skēm), *n.* 1. A plan; a plot. 2. An arrangement.

schol ar ship (skol′ ər ship), *n.* 1. Knowledge acquired by study. 2. Money given to a student for his education.

scoun drel (skoun′ drəl), *n.* A rascal; a person who is cruel or dishonest.

screen (skrēn), *n.* Cloth, wire, netting, or other material mounted on a frame.

screw driv er (skrü′ drī′ vər), *n.* A tool for tightening and loosening screws.

se cret (sē′ krit), *adj.* Kept from the knowledge of others. —*n.* Something known only by a few people; something hidden.

sec tion (sek′ shən), *n.* A part of an object; a division of an organization.

seek (sēk), *v.,* **sought, seeking.** To look for; to hunt; to search for. —**seeker,** *n.* One who seeks.

seize (sēz), *v.* 1. To take by force. 2. To grab.

se mes ter (sə mes′ tər), *n.* Half of a school year; a school term of from 15 to 18 weeks.

sem i an nu al ly (sem′ ē an′ yu̇ ə lē), *adv.* Every six months. [From Latin *semi* half + *annus* year.]

sen ior (sēn′ yər), *adj., abbr.* **Sr.** 1. Distinguishing a father from a son with the same first name. 2. Older. 3. Having to do with the last year in high school or college.

se ñor (sā nyōr′), *n. Spanish.* 1. Mr. 2. A gentleman.

sense (sens), *n.* 1. The ability to understand. 2. Sight, touch, hearing, taste, or smell.

sep a rate (*v.* sep′ ə rāt; *adj.* sep′ ər it, sep′rit), *v.* To put apart; to divide. —*adj.* 1. Not a part of. 2. Apart from others. 3. Single. —**separately,** *adv.* In a way that is not together.

serf (sėrf), *n.* A peasant in a feudal society.

ser geant (sär′ jənt), *n.* 1. A noncommissioned officer in a military organization. 2. A police officer ranking above a patrolman but below a lieutenant.

ser mon (sėr′ mən), *n.* 1. A speech on a religious subject, given in a church. 2. A serious talk about conduct or duty.

serve (sėrv), *v.,* **served.** 1. To work for. 2. To bring food to a table. 3. To be what is needed.

serv ice (sėr′ vis), *n.* 1. A religious meeting or ritual. 2. An act that helps another. —*v.* **serviced, servicing.** To work on; to maintain.

sev enth (sev′ ənth), *adj.* Next after the sixth; last in a series of seven.

sex tet (seks tet′), *n.* Music performed by six instruments or singers; a group of six.

shake (shāk), *v.* To make move up and down or back and forth.

sher iff (sher′ if), *n.* The chief law-enforcing officer in a county.

shield (shēld), *n.* 1. A protector. 2. Armor carried to ward off blows in battle. —*v.* To protect.

shock (shok), *n.* 1. A sudden jolt. 2. A violent surprise.

short age (shôr′ tij), *n.* An insufficient supply.

shoul der (shōl′ dər), *n.* 1. The part of the body of a person or animal where the arm or foreleg joins the body. 2. The part of a coat, dress, etc., at the shoulder. 3. The edge of a road.

shov el (shuv′ əl), *n.* A tool used to dig and to lift and move dirt, snow, or other loose material.

show er (shou′ ər), *n.* 1. A brief rain. 2. A party for giving presents to a person.

show man ship (shō′ mən ship), *n.* Ability to entertain.

shown (shōn), *v., past part.* of **show.** They were *shown* to the door.

side track (sīd′ trak′), *n.* A short track to which railroad cars can be switched.

sig na ture (sig′ nə chər, -chu̇r), *n.* 1. A person's handwritten name; an autograph. 2. in music, a set of signs placed at the beginning of a staff to show the key and time.

si lent (sī′ lənt), *adj.* Without noise.

sim ple (sim′ pəl), *adj.* 1. Easy to do. 2. Not complicated. —**simply,** *adv.* In an easy way.

sin cere ly (sin sir′ lē), *adv.* 1. Earnestly. 2. Honestly. —*Ant.* **dishonestly.**

sin gle (sing′ gəl), *adj.* 1. One. 2. Not married.

si ren (sī′ rən), *n.* A device for making a loud whistle.

smooth (smüᴛʜ), *adj.* Having a very even surface; not rough. —**smoothly,** *adv.* Evenly.

soar (sôr, sōr), *v.* To fly gracefully; to sail upward.

so cial (sō′ shəl), *adj.* 1. Having to do with the relations of people to each other and to society. 2. Friendly; liking company. —**socially,** *adv.* In relation to other people.

sock[1] (sok), *v.* To hit hard. [From Old English *sincan* to sink.]

sock[2] (sok), *n., pl.* **socks.** A short stocking that reaches no higher than the knee. [From Old English *socc* a light slipper.]

so da (sō′ də), *n.* 1. A white substance used in medicine and baking powder. 2. Soda water. 3. A beverage of water to which carbon dioxide and, usually, flavoring have been added.

sol dier (sōl′ jər), *n.* A person serving in an army.

sole[1] (sōl), *n.* 1. The under surface of the foot. 2. The bottom of a shoe or boot. —*v.* To furnish with a sole. Have your shoes *soled.* [From Latin *solea* shoe, from Latin *solum* bottom.]

sole[2] (sōl), *n.* A flatfish that has a small mouth and small eyes set close together. [From Latin *solea* the sole-fish.]

sole[3] (sōl), *adj.* Single; only; one. I was the *sole* heir. [From Latin *solus* alone.]

so lo (sō′ lō), *n., pl.* **solos.** Music performed by one voice or instrument.

so pran o (sə pran′ ō, -prä′ nō), *n.* The part in music sung by the highest singing voice.

sore (sôr, sōr), *adj.* 1. Hurting; causing pain. 2. Irritated. —**sorely,** *adv.* Badly.

soul (sōl), *n.* The spiritual part of a person.

sour (sour), *adj.* 1. Having an acid or tart taste. 2. Spoiled, such as *sour* milk. 3. Unpleasant.

source (sôrs, sōrs), *n.* 1. The beginning of a stream or river. 2. The beginning or origin of something. 3. That which supplies information.

spe cial (spesh′ əl), *adj.* Different from others.

spe cies (spē′ shēz), *n.* 1. Kind; sort; class. 2. In classifying plants and animals, a group with certain characteristics in common.

spe cif ic (spi sif′ ik), *adj.* Definite; precise; particular. —*Syn.* **exact.**

speed (spēd), *v.* To go or cause to go very quickly. —*n.* Haste; quickness. —**speedy,** *adj.* Going quickly. —**speeder,** *n.* One who speeds.

sphere (sfir), *n.* A globe; a ball.

spir it (spir′ it), *n.* The soul; the part of a person that is not the body; a ghost.

sponge (spunj), *n., pl.* **sponges.** 1. Sea animals. 2. The porous material that remains when the living matter has been removed from a sponge.

sports man ship (spôrts′ mən ship, spōrts′-), *n.* 1. Ability in sports. 2. A sense of fair play in sports. We displayed good *sportsmanship.*

sta ble[1] (stā′ bəl), *n.* A building in which horses are kept. —*v.* To put or keep in a stable. [From Latin *stabulum* a standing place.]

sta ble[2] (stā′ bəl), *adj.* 1. Firmly established; not likely to change suddenly. 2. Steady in purpose. [From Latin *stabilis* able to stand.]

sta di um (stā′ dē əm), *n.* A circular or oval structure with seats for spectators of games.

staff (staf, stäf), *n., pl.* **staffs** or **staves.** 1. A pole, stick, or rod used to support or hold up, such as the *staff* of a flag. 2. A body of assistants to a manager. 3. Five horizontal lines with their four spaces, on which music is written.

stake (stāk), *n.* A pointed piece of wood driven into the ground.

starch (stärch), *n.* 1. A white, odorless, tasteless carbohydrate that is an important food element. 2. A preparation of this used to stiffen clothes, etc. —*v.* To stiffen with starch.

sta tion ar y (stā′ shə ner′ ē), *adj.* 1. Permanent. 2. Not moving; staying in one place.

sta tion er y (stā′ shə ner′ ē), *n.* Paper, cards, etc., on which to write.

steam (stēm), *n.* Water in its gaseous state; the gas into which water is converted when boiled.

steel (stēl), *n.* An alloy of iron and other metals.

steep (stēp), *adj.,* **steeper, steepest.** 1. Sloping sharply, almost straight up or down. 2. High.

stock (stok), *v.* To keep on hand; to keep in a store to sell. —*n.* 1. The supply of goods or articles. 2. Livestock. 3. A share in a business.

stock ade (sto kād′), *n.* 1. An enclosure for prisoners; a military prison. 2. An enclosure walled off by posts driven into the ground.

stom ach (stum′ ək), *n.* The part of the body in which food is stored and digested.

straight (strāt), *adj.* 1. Not bending. 2. Orderly.

stress (stres), *n.* 1. Force; pressure. 2. Emphasis.

strike (strīk), *v.,* **struck, striking.** 1. To hit. 2. To remove or cancel. 3. To quit work in order to force some change in the conditions of employment. —*n.* The act of striking.

struck (struk), *v., past* and *past part.* of **strike.** The colonies *struck* a blow for liberty.

struc ture (struk′ chər), *n.* 1. A building; anything that has been built. 2. The way parts are arranged, as in the *structure* of an insect.

PRONUNCIATION KEY: **hat, āge, cãre, fär; let, ēqual, tėrm; it, īce; hot, ōpen, ôrder; oil, out; cup, pu̇t, rüle; child; long; she; thin; ᴛʜen; zh,** measure; ə represents **a** in about, **ə** in taken, **i** in pencil, **o** in lemon, **u** in circus.

stuck (stuk), *v., past* of **stick.** Our car was *stuck* in mud.
stu dent (stü′ dənt, styü′-), *n.* One who goes to school; one who studies.
stuff (stuf), *n.* Any kind of matter.
style (stīl), *n.* Fashion.
sub ject (*v.* səb jekt′; *n.* sub′ jikt), *v.* To cause to undergo. I was *subjected* to an unpleasant experience. —*n.* 1. A course of study. 2. In grammar, the word or phrase about which a statement is made.
sub mit (səb mit′), *v.,* **submitted.** 1. To offer for consideration. 2. To surrender. [From Latin *sub* under + *mittere* to send.]
suc cess (sək ses′), *n.* A favorable outcome. —*Ant.* **failure.**
suc cess ful (sək ses′ fəl), *adj.* Having success; achieving what was worked for. —*Ant.* **unsuccessful.** —**successfully,** *adv.* In a successful way.
sud den (sud′ ən), *adj.* 1. Not expected. 2. Quick. —**suddenly,** *adv.* In a quick way. —**suddenness,** *n.* Quickness.
sue (sü), *v.* To take a person to court.
suf fer (suf′ ər), *v.* To feel pain; to undergo hardship, loss, or unhappiness.
suf fi cient (sə fish′ ənt), *adj.* As much as needed. —*Syn.* **enough.**
sug gest (səg jest′, sə-), *v.* To tell; to tell in an indirect way. —**suggestion,** *n.* A thing suggested.
sup port (sə pôrt′, -pōrt′), *n.* 1. Help; aid. 2. Means by which a person keeps himself or another alive. —**supporter,** *n.* One who supports.
su preme (sə prēm′, sů-), *adj.* Highest; greatest. —*Syn.* **superior.**
sur face (sėr′ fis), *n.* 1. The outside. 2. Top layer. —*v.* To come to the surface of water.
sur round (sə round′), *v.* To encircle.
sus pect (*v.* sə spekt′; *n.* sus′ pekt), *v.* To think something may be true although one is not sure. —*n.* A person who may have committed a crime.
switch yard (swich′ yärd′), *n.* A yard for changing railroad cars from one track to another.
syc a more (sik′ ə môr, -mōr), *n.* A buttonwood tree. *Sycamores* are grown as shade trees.
sym pa thy (sim′ pə thē), *n.* The ability to understand and share another person's feelings. —*Syn.* **pity.**
sys tem (sis′ təm), *n.* A way of doing things. —*Syn.* Method.

T

tab let (tab′ lit), *n.* 1. Sheets of writing paper fastened together at one edge. 2. A pill.
tacks (taks), *n. pl.* Small, sharp nails with large, flat heads.
tank (tangk), *n.* 1. A large container for liquids. 2. A military vehicle covered with armor and running on caterpillar tracks.
tax (taks), *n., pl.* **taxes.** Money paid to a government to pay its expenses; a toll.
tear (tãr), *v.,* **tore, torn.** To pull apart; to rip.
tele-, *prefix.* Far off; at a distance.
tel e graph (tel′ ə graf, -gräf), *n.* An electrical device for sending messages. [From Greek *tele* far off + *graphein* to write.]
tel e phone (tel′ ə fōn), *n.* An instrument for transmitting sound by means of wires and electricity. [From Greek *tele* far off + *phone* sound; speech.]
tem po rar y (tem′ pə rer′ ē), *adj.* Lasting only a short time; short-term; not permanent.
ten nis (ten′ is), *n.* An outdoor game played on a court by players using rackets to hit a ball back and forth over a net.
ter race (ter′ is), *n.* A level space outside a house, often paved and used for living space; a patio.
ter rif ic (tə rif′ ik), *adj.* 1. Causing great fear. 2. Very great. —*Syn.* **frightful.**
that's (ᴛʜats), *contraction.* That is.
the a ter (thē′ ə tər), *n.* A room or building in which plays or motion pictures are featured.
there fore (ᴛʜãr′ fôr, -fōr), *adv.* For that reason.
ther mom e ter (thər mom′ ə tər), *n.* An instrument for measuring temperature. [From Greek *thermos* hot + *metron* measure.]
they've (ᴛʜāv), *contraction.* They have.
throat (thrōt), *n.* The front of the neck.
thus (ᴛʜus), *adv.* In this way; so.
tick et (tik′ it), *n.* A paper or card that allows one to gain admission.
tid al (tī′ dəl), *adj.* Ebbing and flowing like tides.
tight (tīt), *adj.* Firmly stretched.
tim ber (tim′ bər), *n.* Wood used for building.
time ta ble (tīm′ tā′ bəl), *n.* Schedule; something that shows the times when trains, planes, or buses arrive and depart.
tin sel (tin′ səl), *n.* Glittering metal or paper, used as a decoration.
-tion, -ion, -ation, -sion, *n. suffix.* 1. Act of. 2. Result of. 3. State of.

toast (tōst), *n.* A slice of bread that has been browned by heat.

toil (toil), *v.* To work.

to ken (tō′ kən), *n.* 1. A sign; a mark. 2. A piece of metal used in place of a coin.

tone (tōn), *n.* A musical sound; the quality of any sound, its loudness, pitch, etc.

tore (tôr, tōr), *v., past* of **tear.** I *tore* my shirt.

tor na do (tôr nā′ dō), *n.* An extremely violent whirlwind; a destructive windstorm under a funnel-shaped cloud that passes over land in a narrow path.

tor rent (tôr′ ənt, tor′-), *n.* A rushing of water.

to tal (tō′ təl), *n.* The sum; the whole amount. **—totally,** *adv.* In a total and complete way.

tough (tuf), *adj.* Hard to tear or break; strong.

tour na ment (tėr′ nə mənt, tu̇r′-), *n.* 1. A contest involving many participants in sports. 2. In the Middle Ages, a series of duels.

to ward (tôrd, tōrd), *prep.* In the direction of.

tow el (tou′ əl), *n.* Material for drying something.

tow er (tou′ ər), *n.* A high structure, either standing alone or forming part of a building.

trac tor (trak′ tər), *n.* A machine that pulls wagons, plows, etc.

traf fic (traf′ ik), *n.* The passage back and forth of people or vehicles.

trai tor (trā′ tər), *n.* 1. A person who commits treason. 2. A person who betrays another.

trans-, *prefix.* Across.

trans act (tran zakt′, -sakt′), *v.* To attend to; to carry on; to do; to manage.

trans at lan tic (trans′ ət lan′ tik, tranz′-), *adj.* Across the Atlantic Ocean.

trans con ti nen tal (trans′ kon tə nen′ təl), *adj.* Across a continent.

trans fu sion (trans fyü′ zhən), *n.* To take blood from the veins of one person and put it in the veins of another. [From Latin *trans* across + *fusion* joining.]

tran sient (tran′ shənt), *adj.* Passing soon; not lasting. [From Latin *trans* across + *ire* to go.]

trans por ta tion (trans′ pər tā′ shən), *n.* The taking of goods or people from one place to another.

treas ure (trezh′ ər, trā′ zhər), *n.* Thing of value.

tre men dous (tri men′ dəs), *adj.* Very large.

tri an gu lar (trī ang′ gyə lər), *adj.* Shaped like a triangle; having three sides.

tril lion (tril′ yən), *n.* One thousand billion.

trim (trim), *v.,* **trimmed, trimming.** 1. To decorate. 2. To clip; to prune.

tri o (trē′ ō), *n.* Music performed by three voices or three instruments; a group of three. [From Latin *tres* three.]

trom bone (trom′ bōn, trom bōn′), *n.* A large, brass musical instrument with a movable tube that the player slides to produce different tones. [From Italian *tromba* trumpet.]

truck (truk), *n.* Vehicle for carrying loads.

trust (trust), *n.* Confidence; belief. —*Syn.* **faith.**

tur bu lent (tėr′ byə lənt), *adj.* Violent; stormy. *Turbulent* winds accompanied the rain. [From Latin *turba* confusion. Doublet of TROUBLE.]

twelve (twelv), *n.* The cardinal number 12. —*Syn.* **dozen.**

type (tīp), *v.,* **typed, typing.** 1. To typewrite; to use a typewriter. 2. To classify.

ty phoon (tī fün′), *n.* A Pacific storm of violent winds and heavy rain.

U

um pire (um′ pīr), *n.* A person who watches a game to enforce the rules.

un-, *prefix.* Not.

un at tend ed (un′ ə ten′ did), *adj.* 1. Not attended; alone. 2. Not attended to; not cared for.

un com fort a ble (un kumf′ tə bəl, -kum′ fer-), *adj.* Uneasy.

un de cid ed (un′ di sī′ did), *adj.* Not having made up one's mind.

un furled (un fėrld′), *adj.* Unfolded; unrolled.

un ion (yün′ yən), *n.* 1. A coming together. 2. An organization that represents workers in a certain industry; a labor *union.*

up per (up′ ər), *adj.* Having to do with the one that is on top; having to do with the higher one, as an *upper* tooth. —*Ant.* **lower.**

u ra ni um (yu̇ rā′ nē əm), *n.* A chemical element that is a heavy, white, shining substance and is used as a source of atomic energy.

ur ban (ėr′ bən), *adj.* Of or having to do with a city or town, such as an *urban* center. [From Latin *urbs* city.] —*Ant.* **rural.**

u su al ly (yü′ zhu̇ əl ē), *adv.* Almost always.

V

vac u um (vak′ yům, -yů əm), *n.* Empty, even of air. [From Latin *vacuus* empty.]
vain (vān), *adj.* Without success.
vale (vāl), *n.* A valley.
val u a ble (val′ yů ə bəl, -yə bəl), *adj.* Precious; worth a great deal of money.
val ue (val′ yü), *n.* Worth. —*v.* 1. To decide the worth in money. 2. To prize; to think highly of.
vane (vān), *n.* A movable device fastened to a high object to show the wind's direction.
va por (vā′ pər), *n.* 1. Moisture that can be seen in air; fog, clouds, etc. 2. A gas, usually of a substance that is normally solid or liquid.
var i ous (vãr′ ē əs), *adj.* Differing from one another; of different kinds.
var y (vãr′ ē), *v.* To make different; to be different.
vault (vôlt), *n.* A special place where valuable things are kept.
veg e ta ble (vej′ tə bəl, vej′ ə-), *n.* Any plant eaten by humans.
veil (vāl), *n.* 1. Very thin cloth worn over the face. 2. Anything that partially conceals.
vein (vān), *n.* A continuous crack in the earth's rock, filled with a mineral.
view (vyü), *n.* 1. Sight; the act or power of seeing. 2. A scene.
vi o lent (vī′ ə lənt), *adj.* 1. Given to sudden force. 2. Striking suddenly and angrily. —*Ant.* **calm.**
vi o lin (vī′ ə lin′), *n.* A musical instrument whose bow is drawn across its strings.
vo cab u lar y (vō kab′ yə ler′ ē), *n.* The stock of words used in a language.

W

waist (wāst), *n.* The small part of the body above the hips.
-ward, -wards, *suffix.* Leading to.
ward en (wôr′ dən), *n.* 1. One in charge of a prison. 2. A person who enforces laws of hunting and fishing; a game *warden.*
ware house (wãr′ hous′), *n.* A place for storage.
weak (wēk), *adj.* Not strong.
wealth (welth), *n.* Riches; the state of having much money or property. —**wealthy,** *adj.* Having much money.
weath er (weᴛʜ′ ər), *n.* The atmospheric conditions of air.
weave (wēv), *v.* To make threads into cloth, usually on a loom.
weight (wāt), *n.* Amount of heaviness.
wel fare (wel′ fãr′), *n.* 1. The state of being well. 2. The extent to which a whole country is well. [From *well* + *fare.*]
we've (wēv), *contraction.* We have.
what ev er (hwot ev′ ər, hwət-), *pron.* 1. Anything that. 2. No matter what.
wheth er (hweᴛʜ′ ər), *conj.* 1. Used to denote a choice. 2. If.
whirl wind (hwėrl′ wind′), *n.* A wind blowing in a circular pattern.
whole (hōl), *adj.* All; complete. —**wholly,** *adv.* Mainly; entirely.
whom (hüm), *pron.* 1. What person? 2. Which person?
will ing (wil′ ing), *adj.* Ready; wanting to; not refusing to. —*Ant.* **unwilling.**
wire (wīr), *n.* A threadlike strand of metal.
with in (wiᴛʜ in′, with-), *prep.* Inside.
wolf (wůlf), *n., pl.* **wolves.** A wild mammal related to the dog.
won der (wun′ dər), *n.* 1. Something extraordinary; a marvel. 2. The feeling of great astonishment. —*v.* 1. To feel surprise or astonishment. 2. To have some doubt and curiosity.
wres tle (res′ əl), *n.* A physical contest in which the contestants try to throw each other down.
wrist (rist), *n.* The joint between the hand and the arm.

Y

-y[1], *adj. suffix.* 1. Having. 2. Being like.
-y[2], *n. suffix.* State of.
yard mas ter (yärd′ mas′ tər, -mäs′-), *n.* A person in charge of a railroad yard.
year ly (yir′ lē), *adj.* Every year. —*Syn.* **annually.**
yell (yel), *v.* To cry out in a loud voice. —*Syn.* **scream.**
yolk (yōk), *n.* The yellow part of an egg.
you're (yůr), *contraction.* You are. *You're* here early.
your self (yůr self′, yər-), *pron., pl.* **yourselves.** A form of *you* used for emphasis. You *yourself* made this.

a b c d e f g h i

j k l m n o p q r

s t u v w x y z

HANDWRITING MODELS

Upward loop letters b e f h k l

Oval letters a c d g o q

Rounded letters m n v x y z

Pointed letters i j p r s t u w

A B C D E F G H I

J K L M N O P Q R

S T U V W X Y Z

Writing by: P. Z. Bloser

GLOSSARY OF SPELLING TERMS

abbreviation A shortened form of a word, such as *Mr. P. 78*

antonyms Words that have opposite meanings. *Urban* and *rural* are antonyms. *P. 25*

apostrophe The mark (') used in a contraction to show where one or more letters have been omitted. The apostrophe is also used to show possession. *Pp. 78, 79*

base word A word that has no prefix or suffix. The simplest form of a word. The base word in *listed* is *list. P. 3*

closed syllable A syllable that ends with a consonant, such as the first syllable in *postpone. P. 14*

compound A word that is formed from two or more words, such as *lifeguard* or *high school. Pp. 22, 78*

consonant A sound, such as /t/ or /sh/, that is not a vowel. *P. 2*

consonant cluster Two or more consonant sounds with no vowel sound between, such as /st/ in *steep. P. 8*

contraction A word such as *hasn't*. An apostrophe is used in place of the omitted letter or letters. *P. 78*

derived form A word form that is a different part of speech from the base word. *Convention* is a derived form of *convene. P. 47*

digraph Two adjoining letters that spell a single sound, such as *ai* in *main* or *ea* in *deal. P. 5*

diphthong A speech sound that is a blended vowel, such as /oi/ in *avoid. P. 30*

double letters Two letters together that are alike, such as *rr* in *barrel. P. 43*

doublets Two different words that come from the same source, such as *guard* and *ward. P. 25*

entry word A word that is defined in a dictionary. *P. 116*

guide words The two words at the top of a dictionary page. They tell the first and last words on the page. *P. 116*

homographs Words such as *present* (pri zent') and *present* (prez' ənt). Homographs are spelled alike but have different meanings and sometimes different pronunciations. *Pp. 34, 100*

homophones Words such as *waste* and *waist*. Homophones sound alike but have different meanings and different spellings. *Pp. 6, 97*

open syllable A syllable that ends with a vowel, such as the first syllable in *navy. P. 5*

plural A word that stands for more than one of something. *Radios* is the plural form of *radio. P. 15*

possessive A form of a word that shows ownership, such as *man's* hat. *P. 79*

prefix A letter, or letters, used at the beginning of a base word to form another word. The *un* in *uncertain* is a prefix. *P. 25*

respelling The second spelling of a dictionary entry word. In a respelling, symbols are used to show what sound a word has. *P. 6*

schwa A vowel sound, shown by the symbol ə, in weak syllables. *P. 12*

stress mark The mark used in a dictionary respelling to show a syllable that is said with force. Some words have two stressed syllables. The **primary stress mark** (′) shows the syllable with greater stress; the **secondary stress mark** (′) shows the syllable with less stress, as in the word *incorrect* (in′ kə rekt′). *Pp. 9, 91*

suffix A letter, or letters, added to the end of a base word. The *ed* in *listed* is a suffix. *P. 3*

syllable Each part of a word that has a vowel. *P. 2*

synonyms Words that have almost the same meanings. *Dozen* and *twelve* are synonyms. *P. 3*

vowel A sound that is usually spelled with one or more of these letters: *a, e, i, o, u, y. P. 2*